D0862565

Edgar Allan Poe

Edgar Allan Poe
Brian Morton

HAUS PUBLISHING • LONDON

First published in Great Britain in 2010 by
Haus Publishing Ltd
70 Cadogan Place
London SW1X 9AH
www.hauspublishing.com

Copyright © Brian Morton, 2010

The moral right of the author has been asserted

A CIP catalogue record for this book
is available from the British Library

ISBN 978-1-905791-52-1

Typeset in Sabon by MacGuru Ltd
Printed in the United States of America

CONDITIONS OF SALE
All rights reserved. No part of this publication may be reproduced,
stored in a retrieval system, or transmitted in any form or by any means,
electronic, mechanical, photocopying, recording or otherwise, without
the prior permission of the publisher.

This book is sold subject to the condition that it shall not, by way of
trade or otherwise, be lent, re-sold, hired out or otherwise circulated
without the publisher's prior consent in any form of binding or cover
other than that in which it is published and without a similar condition
including this condition being imposed on the subsequent purchaser.

Contents

Introduction   1

1. "Let me call myself, *for the present*": Poe's early life, 1809–1811   11

2. "Not a Spark of affection for us": Poe and his foster family, 1811–20   23

3. "The most dissolute university of Europe": Poe and further education, 1820–29   39

4. "A dream within a dream": Poe's early work, 1829–31   54

5. "PS I am poor": Poe and the literary life, 1831–6   71

6. "My darling little wifey": Poe and Virginia, 1836–9   91

7. "Ill-conceived and miserably executed": Poe as editor and critic, 1839–42   106

8. "Long intervals of horrible sanity": Poe's short stories, 1842–44   124

9. "We peer into the abyss": Poe's decline, 1844–6   141

10. "To the few who love me and whom I love": Poe's later work, 1846–8   155

11. "I must die": Poe's final year, 1848–49   170

Chronology   182

Index   193

Introduction

It is either the most pompous or the most elegant put-down in the history of cultural criticism. In his influential three-volume *Main Currents in American Thought* (1928), Vernon Louis Parrington dismisses the work of Edgar Allan Poe in its entirety as "the atrabilious wretchedness of the dipsomaniac". Leaving aside the lofty tone, it is a difficult verdict to counter. Poe was a drunk; his behaviour was frequently abject; and his work often appears to be steeped in black bile. Also, given Parrington's methodology and premises in *Main Currents*, one would not expect him to give Poe a sympathetic reading. At the very outset, Parrington promises to "eschew belletristic triflings" and to concentrate on the history of American political and social ideas rather than polite literature. Even setting aside their content, the very forms in which Poe specialised – the short story, lyric poem and the sketch – were liable to put Parrington off. Few, though, have been able to set aside Poe's obsession with the dark and morbid, with romantic agonies and sexual perversity, genetic fatality and irrationality, none of which squared at all comfortably with Parrington's model of American history as firstly Puritan, but then Enlightened and Progressive. Finally, one would have to say that the two men seem at first glance to be divided by vast differences of physical temperament. As well as being the doyen – some might say the founder – of American studies, Parrington was also a distinguished football coach, happiest in the open air and with team effort. It is worthwhile making an early distinction between Poe and his creations because the consensus tends to conflate them, but the characters at least are almost all neurasthenic solitaries, consumptive or otherwise unrobust, disgusted by physical contact, incapable of strenuous movement. Lurking behind Parrington's dismissal is the feeling that Poe was somehow un-American.

The idea of Poe as alien, estranged, something got up "for French eyes" is a beguiling and persistent one. In critical terms, he owes his reputation largely to the admiration of Stephane Mallarme (who wrote a much-anthologised eulogy on "Le Tombeau d'Edgar Poe") and to Charles Baudelaire (whose translation of Poe's only finished novel *The Narrative of Arthur Gordon Pym* begins with an extraordinary linguistic homage) and to D. H. Lawrence (who puts Poe in a key position in his *Studies in Classic American Literature*, published in England in 1923, half a decade before Parrington's book). Of his countrymen, writing in that same decade of experiment, only the poet William Carlos Williams – significantly, a kind of "offshore American" has much positive to say about Poe, devoting the last full chapter of his 1925 meditation *In The American Grain* to his work and offering in it some of the best and most practical insights we have.

Williams saw what Parrington could not. "Poe gives the sense for the first time in America that literature is *serious*, not a matter of courtesy but of truth." Williams' Poe is that utterly American thing, a pioneer, the work a single, undifferentiated gesture which from its choices of subject, the inclusion of philosophy *and* trivia, right to the inner structure of the sentences "is a movement, first and last, to clear the GROUND".

It is tempting to resort to word-play and suggest that, Williams' repositioning of him aside, Poe tends to work *against* the American grain, his inclusiveness and language experiments, his themes and obsessions radically different to those of, say, Walt Whitman, who seems a poet of the open air and strong light rather than incense-laden rooms lit with guttering candles, whose optimistic democracy contrasts sharply with Poe's aristocratic elitism, and whose poetic style has a more obvious influence on subsequent generations. More obvious, but not necessarily more profound. Not least in order to let V. L. Parrington return to the rest Poe's restless creations are denied, it might be possible to play on his title as well and say that far from being a marginal figure, Edgar Allan Poe represents one of the main *under*currents in American thought, stirring a dark subterranean tide of ideas and conjectures that would not receive fuller theoretical explication until Freud published *The Interpretation of Dreams* and *The Psychopathology of Everyday Life*, his methods strikingly modern, even post-modern, his most exuberantly speculative fugues sometimes even anticipating the most radical ideas of contemporary science.

ooooo

One of the reasons Poe remains something of an enigma – and it is worth establishing the point before looking at the broad contours of his thought and influence and at what might be called the "Poe myth" – is that he seems not just *sui generis* as a writer but to exist out of time as a man as well.

Casual readers, and those who simply know him by reputation or through screen adaptations of his work, are vague about his dates and speak of him as if he were a late 19th century figure, a contemporary perhaps of Arthur Conan Doyle and Jules Verne, both of whom actually owe him an ancestral debt.

The dates are, of course, pitiably close together. Edgar Allan Poe lived just forty years, which even without the travails he underwent would make the extent of the output particularly impressive. More important in the present context, though, Poe lived and worked in a young country. In 1809, the year of his birth, the United States had been in existence for less than thirty-five years. The nation still largely consisted of the original thirteen colonies plus Ohio, but just as Poe was coming into the world the incorporation of the Indiana and Illinois Territories extended United States influence round the shores of the Great Lakes. The Louisiana Purchase, negotiated with France six years earlier in 1803, was opening up a huge tract of continental heartland. Florida and the entire South West were still Spanish.

James Madison was president. One of the Founding Fathers, he owed his election success to a shrewd grasp of foreign policy. He needed it. The old colonising power, having destroyed the French navy at Trafalgar, was now blockading the American coast, as well as providing arms and support to the dispossessed Native American tribes around the lakes. The two countries would shortly be at war.

Such events might seem of remote significance to the infant Poe but the ebb and flow of Atlantic fortunes were part of his birthright and also central to his orphaned childhood. An ancestor had sailed on the *Mayflower*, and the stepfather from whom Edgar took his middle name was closely involved in the

Atlantic trade. In the year of Waterloo, the six-year-old Poe was beginning his schooling in Irvine, Scotland, John Allan's birthplace: the detail helpfully reinforces both the chronology and the unexpectedly complex geography of his life.

Poe was born in Boston, but we instinctively think of him as Southern. The word helpfully invites a pairing with "Gothic", but it also locates the budding poet in a society which was steadily separating, in economics and custom, from the North. The final decade of the 18th century had seen the introduction of Eli Whitney's cotton gin, which made plantation slavery an economic imperative at a time when the northern states were – more or less altruistically – banning slaveholding. In 1808, the first year such legislation was possible under the terms of the Constitution, Congress abolished the importation of slaves, an initiative which did not in any sense bring to an end the "peculiar institution" but further sharpened diverging attitudes to it.

It is no coincidence that the closing cadence of Williams's *In The American Grain* should begin with an essay on "The Advent of the Slaves". Between that and the essay on Poe is a short piece on the fatal glamour of the primitive, sparked by the story of one John Houston, Scotch-Irish like Poe himself, who ran away to join the Cherokee and live in a state of nature. Williams ends it with a paragraph that chimes closely with his already-quoted comments on Poe: " ... we have no other choice: we must go back to the beginning: it must all be done over; everything that is must be destroyed". Race, colour, subservience, dread of, and attraction to, "the Other", death and apocalypse: these were part of Poe's genetic imprint.

ooooo

Poe grew up, then, in a young and in many respects primitive country, founded in the Word and the law, but still conspicuously lawless and unliterary, if not illiterate. When Poe began publishing in the early 1820s, "American literature" did not exist in any meaningful sense. In literary taste, if not in politics, the new republic was still largely in thrall to the old colonial power, a situation that was encouraged by the absence of binding copyright; new titles published in London were simply pirated on their arrival in New York or Baltimore. The American newspaper and magazine press, which Poe came to know intimately as an insider, was vociferous at best, crude at worst, a vehicle for invective, black propaganda and scandal rather than delicate prose or disinterested analysis.

Of the major 19th century American writers, the only ones substantially older than Poe were Charles Brockden Brown (1771–1810), who in *Wieland* (1798) and other inferior novels tried to Americanise the Gothic form; Washington Irving (1783–1859), creator of Rip Van Winkle and the first American writer to gain an international reputation; and, most importantly, James Fenimore Cooper (1789–1851), in whose "Leatherstocking" tales D. H. Lawrence detected the creation of a more sanguine American myth; William Gilmore Simms (1806–70) was his Southern equivalent. These were the writers who might overturn the universal vogue for Sir Walter Scott.

Of a later generation Herman Melville (1819–91), author of *Moby-Dick,* was ten years younger, as was the poet Walt Whitman (1819–1892). Nathaniel Hawthorne (1804–1864) was half a decade older, admittedly, but did not begin to publish until 1837, when his *Twice-Told Tales* – given a mixed review in the *Broadway Journal* by one Edgar Allan Poe – gathered together work that had previously appeared in magazines. Hawthorne sent a copy to another target of Poe's animosity, the poet Henry Wadsworth Longfellow (1807–1882), who had recently identified the thinness of American letters to date and called out for distinguished and distinctive writing in the United States.

Longfellow served nearly two decades as professor of French and Spanish at Harvard, a reminder that there had been a time when it was far from inevitable that a new "American" literature would be written in English. Longfellow's successor in the post was James Russell Lowell (1818–1891) who in the year before Poe's death published his own satirical survey of American letters in *A Fable for Critics* (1848). It contains the devastating couplet: "There comes Poe, with his raven, like Barnaby Rudge, / Three fifths of him genius and two fifths sheer fudge." It was an estimate that stuck for nearly a century.

Of an older generation, Philip Freneau (1752–1832), a now seldom-read writer of satirical and declamatory verse as well as more meditative pieces, was by 1809 largely sidetracked into politics; of published Freneau biographies, two bear the equally telling subtitles *Poet of the Revolution* and *A Study in Literary Failure*. The only senior figure of real creative standing was William Cullen Bryant (1794–1878), whose "To A Waterfowl", written in 1815 when just out of his teens, was deemed by Matthew Arnold to be the most perfect lyric in the language and thus a potential model for Poe, though it is marked by the same allegorical strain Poe condemned in Hawthorne's stories.

Attempting to provide some philosophical underpinning for an emergent American literature was the poet and essayist Ralph Waldo Emerson (1803–82), whose definitive statement appeared as *Nature* in 1836. Emerson's ideas, which came to define the movement known as Transcendentalism, were European importations, the philosophy of Immanuel Kant as popularised by Samuel Taylor Coleridge and Thomas Carlyle. It was left to Henry David Thoreau (1817–62) in his classic *Walden* (1856) to give Transcendentalism a distinctively American spin.

Significantly, all of these men – with the exception of Freneau and Brown – outlived Poe, in some cases by many decades. Inevitably, this meant that they experienced at first hand the vast social and economic disruptions of the Civil War, a trauma which Poe seemed to anticipate and foreshadow. *His* transcendentalism had a dark aspect. What he unquestionably had in common with these writers, over and above certain shared concerns, was the simple struggle to be a writer in a society and economy which had not yet reached the necessary critical mass or level of civil society to support polite literature. Melville's struggles to make a living are well-known – his cry "Oh, time, strength, cash, patience!" has become a motto for struggling authors – but Poe's are even more heroic, given his circumstances. In a country where political sovereignty was still fluid and under question – states' rights versus federal government being the insistent bass note – it was unlikely that America could sustain a cultural "establishment" of the European sort. The pre-literary world in which he operated was brutally competitive, almost feral.

In terms of American writing, Poe is at the beginning of things, his career almost always expressed in terms of potential rather than achievement. One might say of Poe, more than almost any other writer, that the life can only be understood through the work, and the work only through the life, but it is precisely at that treacherous point where they come together that understanding usually surrenders to mythology.

Even though his body of work is out of all reasonable proportion to his actual lifespan, it has been routinely overtaken by
an elaborate personal myth. Every educated American can
recite "The Raven", but even non-poetry readers know that,
like rock and roller Jerry Lee Lewis, Poe married a 13 year old
girl (and just to cap the story with a Gothic twist, his 13 year
old cousin); almost no one has paused long enough to wonder
what was really behind that strange liaison, though its significance seems plain enough when straightforwardly examined.
Few even devoted readers manage to get through the long
essay meditation *Eureka* (Poe himself considered it a prose
poem), but everyone seems to have heard the rumour that
Poe may have died of rabies, or was murdered. His drinking
is remembered, but his initial success as a non-commissioned
officer in the American military is not. His acidulous and
often *ad hominem* reviews of others are often quoted, less so
his generous praise of adventurous contemporaries.

It is always difficult to keep in view, so preposterous a situation does it seem, that much of what we think we know
about Poe stems from a single obituary written by a sworn
enemy, a hack called Rufus Griswold, who subsequently and
by subterfuge became his enemy's literary executor. Griswold
is a chilling forerunner of the modern "unauthorised" biographer, who presents his subject not so much warts-and-all as
mostly warts, but in this case with nakedly personal agenda.
Griswold's professional jealousy led him not just to denigrate
Poe the man but also to devalue the surviving body of writing,
which Griswold as executor ostensibly represented.

Though Poe's (mostly short) work has been sufficiently
well-anthologised to keep it in view – "The Raven" is arguably the stereotypical "anthology poem" – it is work that is
perhaps only properly understood in its entirety. There is a

wholeness to Poe's body of writing that jars strikingly with the unwholesomeness of his life and many of his ideas. The most influential of these jostle with the most controversial. He insisted that the very idea of a long poem was a contradiction in terms and that a lyric poem should be calculated to convey a single mood or impression; this is what he claimed to have done with "The Raven", for which he wrote the final stanza first. Poe also notoriously stated that the most poetic subject was the death of a beautiful woman. Disease, neurasthenia, madness, morbidity, entombment, necrophilia haunt his work like bass notes and dissonant chords, and yet the verve and structural virtuosity with which these dark elements are put together are rarely commented on.

Poe's dissolution was not so much the engine of his genius as its cost. Few great artists have paid so high a price for their art. In what follows, the wholeness of his achievement is the counterweight to personal disaster. Even if Parrington's stern strictures cannot quite be overturned, it might be possible to adjust the proportions in Lowell's back-handed compliment.

1

"Let me call myself, *for the present*": Poe's early life, 1809–1811

Poe's dipsomania and the undoubted wretchedness that came in its wake may have a simple and depressingly familiar origin in the peculiar culture of his upbringing. As readers of *Nicholas Nickleby* will know, it was the habit among theatrical families to give babies and small children spoonsful of gin or whisky in their milk, either to prolong the careers of infant prodigies by stunting their growth or more practically to keep babies asleep and silent backstage while their parents trod the boards. Research proves that early introduction to alcohol often leads to abusive drinking in adult life, and while there is no direct evidence that Poe was "dosed" in this way, the practice was so widespread in the theatre that it is hard to imagine he was an exception.

Though it is harder to trace the origins of an idea, Poe's notorious insistence that the death of a beautiful woman was *the* poetic subject might almost as easily be traced to the early loss not just of the mother who bore him and perhaps tinctured his milk with spirits, but also of a beloved "step-mother". The severed maternal bond was the fundamental fact of Poe's life. It explains his obsession with female mortality and it drove his attention-seeking wilfulness and his often desperate desire to be nurtured. Examine from this perspective what is arguably the most notorious moment of his life – his marriage to 13 year old Virginia Clemm – and one wonders whether the real bond and the real urging was towards Virginia's mother, his unattainable aunt.

It matters more than usual, given his lifelong absorption in matters of blood, to understand what Poe may have taken in with his mother's milk and from his father's genes. The Poes are as frustrating to the biographer as they are fascinating. Of the private life, we know nothing, beyond worrisome hints of the family's hand-to-mouth existence; ironically, though, and particularly so at a time and in a place where ordinary people were little documented, we know a great deal about their brief public life, which was passed in the sputter and glare of limelight.

The future mother of Edgar Poe made her stage debut at the age of nine. Elizabeth Arnold had been brought from England to New England in the late winter of 1796. Four months later, she was lisping her way through "The Market Lass" at the old Boston Theatre. It was her mother's benefit night, when the theatre community, both before and behind the lights, dipped deeper into its pockets to help out a favourite actor or performer. A decade later, Eliza Hopkins and Eliza Poe, as she successively was, would receive benefits of her own and of mixed success, recognised as wife, widow and mother, but always as a particular favourite of the crowd.

The only surviving likeness of Eliza suggests a tiny frame – her son was variously described but seems to have been of below average height – and below the curls that straggle out from under her bonnet, she wears a sweetly unrefined expression

that would have been well-suited to *ingénue* parts, shepherd-
esses and other pastoral roles, like the "Country Lass" in Morton's *Speed the Plough* or Priscilla Tomboy in Bickerstaffe's
The Romp. Even so, Eliza's final appearance before death took
her was as Countess Wintersen in *The Stranger* and she had
along the way played Ophelia, Cordelia, Regan, Juliet, Desde-
mona, Ariel, the Prince of Wales in *Richard III*, Prince John in
Henry IV, Part One, as well as Lydia Languish in *The Rivals*
and other relatively canonical works. It is estimated that in her
short career and leaving aside singing and dancing parts she
performed more than 200 roles. There is nothing much in her
appearance to suggest the famous son (who lived into the photographic age and left one striking daguerreotype); nothing
except the eyes, which reach out of even a miniature portrait
with remarkable intensity and strength.

Strong she must have been. In the same 1801–1802 Philadelphia season, that saw her "Country Lass" and Priscilla,
the fifteen-year-old performed no less than 27 different roles
between October and March and at least 67 separate performances, often singing and dancing as well as acting. It
was an itinerant lifestyle. With her mother, on her own, and
with her successive husbands, Eliza acted in Boston, Port-
land (Maine). Newport (Rhode Island), Charleston (South
Carolina), Wilmington (North Carolina), Philadelphia, Baltimore, Washington, Norfolk and Richmond (Virginia) and
New York. Travel was hazardous and uncomfortable and the
typical American city in summer, when theatres were dark and
money too scarce for medical help, were rife with typhoid and
cholera; fear of contagion was not simply an idiosyncrasy of
Edgar's. In terms of public opinion, the theatre was subject to
a gross double standard. The public was happy to pay for its
entertainment while actors, and particularly actresses, were

treated with considerable disdain, the latter regarded as being just one social rung up from common prostitutes.

With a disregard for polite convention, though also through financial necessity, Eliza continued to perform through all her pregnancies. There is even a record that suggests she was on stage on the evening of January 20 1809, less than twenty four hours after the birth of her second son Edgar, but this can probably be discounted or considered one of the few engagements she failed to make in her short career. Before her marriage and in the absence of her mother (who simply disappears from view and may have fallen victim to one of many epidemics), she was chaperoned and generally taken care of by a Mrs Snowden and by this widowed lady's future husband. He was to bequeath Edgar Allan Poe a name for one of his most celebrated characters and stories, though whether the real Mr Usher suffered the same hypersensitivities and ailments isn't recorded; perhaps he was a bluff and carnal fellow, and the borrowed name was Poe's private joke.

One of her specialities seems to have been vocal after-pieces. These were a throwback to the Elizabethan and Jacobean theatre where it would not have been unknown for the stage to have been cleared of *Hamlet*'s or *King Lear*'s pile of bodies in order for a jig or comic song to be performed. In the last days of 1799, back in Philadelphia after a run in Baltimore, she took part in a special event in memory of George Washington, founding president of the Republic, who had died on December 14; further reminder of how close Poe's life bordered on America's beginnings.

Somewhere around this time, but certainly in Philadelphia, she met an up and coming comic actor called Charles Hopkins. Like most male members of his profession, he seems to have nursed ambitions to play the Prince of Denmark (and may even have achieved them) but his speciality was roles like Tony Lumpkin, the lovable scamp in Oliver Goldsmith's *She Stoops to Conquer*. Charles and Eliza were married sometime in the summer of 1802; unlike her second marriage, no bond survives in the public record. She then joined her husband in Green's Virginia Company. On August 11 (the latest date possible for the marriage) she appears as "Mrs Hopkins" for the first time, though subsequent billings as "late Miss Arnold of Philadelphia" are testimony to her reputation.

She was 16, or maybe still only 15, and destined to be a widow before she was out of her teens. Hopkins died on October 26 1805. The Virginia Company gave a benefit at the Washington Theatre two weeks later. The season closed a few days before Christmas, but Eliza was back on stage at the beginning of the 1806 spring season. It is unwise to read too much into the theatrical record, but apart from a "hornpipe and song" at the end of the January 25th performance back in Richmond there are fewer mentions of songs and dances, not so many fandangos, gavots or minuets de la cour in her credits after the turn of that year. It is as if this young girl has acquired in grief a new dramatic authority.

The rest of her life can be told as briefly as it was. She remarried without much delay, bore three children – one drunk, one poet and storyteller, also a drunk, and one feeble-minded girl – and then died in a Richmond rooming house at the age of 24. Nothing much is known about the circumstances of her death but in the event it was not unexpected. Some two weeks before, her company had announced a special benefit, aware that previous ones had not been as well subscribed as had been hoped. This appeal was a blatant attempt to milk theatregoers' sympathy, either that or it was made in full knowledge of the seriousness of her condition:

"To the Humane Heart – On this night, *Mrs Poe*, lingering on the bed of disease and surrounded by her children, asks your assistance and *asks it perhaps for the last time.*" Some two weeks after her death, the Richmond Theatre burned down, perhaps inconsolable at the loss of such a bright star, perhaps a beyond-the-grave revenge on a public whose generosity was short-measured.

Obituary notices often gloss over former criticisms but Eliza's were consistent with the mostly very good notices she had received, praising her grace, sweetness of expression and acting ability. None of these things was ever redeemable as financial security for what had already become a father-less family. Those children who had been posed round the deathbed would rely on others for their care and upbringing, though it is hard to tell whether Eliza was denied the bless-ing or the curse of seeing feckless Henry, troubled Edgar and poor, distracted Rosalie grown up. To the future poet, she was present more as an ideal than as a real memory, and perhaps he carried with him some pre-verbal imprint of separation, the physical sensation of being consigned to one or another unfamiliar bosom as his mother went off to meet her public. All she could bequeath him, as Arthur Dobson Quinn, the doyen of Poe biographers, observed in 1940, was "her high heart, her unremitting industry, and that indefinable charm which made her a favourite from Boston to Charleston ..."

ooooo

If only the boy had received half as much or half as postive from David Poe. Edgar's father disappears from the story even earlier than Eliza does. On October 18 1809, he played Captain Cypress in Richard Leigh's *Grievings's a Folly* at the

Park Theatre in New York. It was his last curtain call; though he lived for another seven years, Mr Poe does not appear in the record again, a career cut short by "indisposition", which at the time usually meant drunkenness.

History has not been kind to David Poe, who perhaps deserves better than the walk-on part he has been given in most biographies of his son. Edgar liked to hint that there was aristocratic blood in his veins. The reality was more prosaic, though Celtic blood (a few sources add Jewish ancestry to the mix, though this is fanciful) may explain some of the phantasms that stalk his imagination. A John Poe emigrated to America around 1750 from Dring in Co Cavan, Ireland. He brought with him a son, David Sr, who became a spinning wheel maker in Baltimore and a fiery Whig. When the War of Independence began, David Poe Sr joined a local militia and was subsequently appointed Assistant Quartermaster General, with the rank of major. Despite that, he was known for the rest of his life as "General" Poe and remembered for having won the gratitude of the Marquis de LaFayette, a revolutionary hero on both sides of the Atlantic. In 1824, LaFayette made a brief visit to the "General"'s grave, murmuring respectfully "*Ici reste un coeur noble*"; among the honour guard was the 15-year-old Edgar Allan Poe, a lieutenant of cadets. Ironically, it was *Mrs* Poe's heroic needlework that really merited the Marquis's thanks, for single-handedly cutting and turning out 500 pairs of uniform breeches. "General" Poe also saw action in 1814, when the British attacked Baltimore. Ironically, just a year later his grandson would be on British soil and beginning a Scots and English education.

The poet's father, David Jr, was born in Baltimore on July 18 1784. There was no theatre in the family background, beyond, that is, the "General"'s obvious talent for self-dram-atisation. However, at the age of 19, he turned his back on the law and entered a profession that at the time included very few native-born Americans. David Poe's first part was apparently as a soldier in Kotzebue's *La Peyrouse*. That was on December 1 1803. We can be fairly sure that this was his debut, since his next appearance, four days later and again with Placide's Company at the Charleston Theater, was advertised as "Being his second appearance on any stage". This time he played Laertes, but in Brooke's now obscure *Gustavus Vasa* rather than *Hamlet*; his Shakespearean debut came the following week, as Donalbain in the Scottish play. Perhaps to the relief of the senior Poe family, he did not appear in his native Baltimore until the middle of 1805 and in a one-off tryout.

History has not been kind to David Poe. While his young wife has been presented as the darling of the Southern stage, David has been largely dismissed. Nevertheless, he was the target of some fairly venomous criticism. Reviews particu-larly mention his tendency to gabble speeches and complaints about his diction were frequent. Whether these were intended as indirect accusations of drunkenness is not clear, but a bizarre poem published in *Ramblers' Magazine* not long before David's final disappearance from the scene drives the point home. It seems that his surname was regularly punned, from a "*Poh!*" of disgust to the more lavatorial humour of the poem, which was headed "Sur un POE de chambre". The verse also continue in French and end with these cruel lines: "Monsieur Poh n'eut l'empreinte / Son pere etait pot, / Sa mere etait broc [jug] / Sa grand-mere etait pinte." The impli-cation is clear enough.

Two points ought to be made about David Poe's reputation.

First and more generally, journalistic standards at the time were markedly different to now; criticism was often *ad hominem* and bruising, as Edgar was to discover – and practise – later. Three generations of Poe men, from the robustly Whiggish grandfather down to the adversarial poet, were embroiled in squabbles in the public prints. What distinguished David Poe from much of his profession was how very personally he took bad notices. There is evidence that on one occasion, possibly drunk, he went to the home of a distinguished critic and threatened to beat him. What makes the story more interesting and salutary is that the bad review in question was not directed at him but at Eliza. It is be wrong to leave standing an impression of David as constantly howled down while his wife was constantly garlanded. She had her share of criticism as well, though in fairness most of it was based on the unsuitability of certain roles relative to her natural abilities and almost all of it expressed in the most generous and forgiving of terms. His record as an actor, during his short career, was a familiar enough mix of obscure comic roles and minor Shakespearean parts. On April 21 1809, he again played Laertes, but this time in *Hamlet* and opposite his wife's Ophelia, a part some critics felt was beyond her reach.

We know nothing of the Poes' courtship and marriage beyond their appearance on the same stages. Was it an act of gallantry of David's part to offer his hand to an unprotected young widow, or did he hope to win from her some reflected admiration? Whatever the motivation, six months after Charles Hopkins' death Eliza and David were man and wife. Until 1941, no one was clear as to the exact date, but Quinn discovered the marriage bond, made out on March 14 1806, but misfiled with 1800 documents because the clerk had too hastily scrawled the last numeral of the date.

Whatever troubles lay ahead of them – David's drunkenness, Eliza's confinements and declining health, and the interruption of income these would have led to – the bottom line of their married lives was money. The 1806–7 season was cripplingly busy, with nearly 70 performances by the pair, often together but with David carrying most of the weight during late January and early February. The reason was plain enough. On January 30 1807, the Poes became parents. William Henry (possibly also known as Leonard) came into the world in a Boston winter, seemed later to infect his brother with unattainable dreams of exploration and travel, surfaced in occasional letters and mostly in worrisome terms to do with drink or money, and then drifted out again, dead at 24 and so little remarked that a solitary newspaper notice referred to him as "W. H. Pope".

Having a child must have put additional pressure on the Poes' finances. They received a benefit on May 22 and again in April 1808, though the latter occasion, shared with the Ushers, was presented as a means of redressing the "great failure and severe losses sustained by their former attempts". The reason for Eliza Poe's absences that winter is plain. Edgar Poe was born on January 19 1809, also in Boston. Along with her high heart, charm and appetite for hard work, his mother later left him a little drawing of Boston Harbour, inscribed to her son as a representation of his birthplace and "where his mother found her best, and most sympathetic friends". Perhaps the boy later found out too much about those failed benefits; he never showed a scrap of affection for his native town and was reluctant to spend time there.

David Poe seems to have left him little on his departure than a cross-grained and disputatious nature, a thirst for alcohol, and a tendency when asking for help to veer between self-pity and threat. Though the provenance isn't entirely clear, and is only quoted in a second letter, David seems to have approached his cousin George Clemm (a branch of family that will be of considerable importance later) to wheedle a loan. The tone is extraordinary, in itself and because it so much anticipates Edgar's own later importunings of John Allan. It seems David first went to the house and left a message with a servant, insisting on meeting George the next day at the Mansion House. The appointment was obviously not kept and the subsequent letter is full of angry hurt, promising as a point of honour which it is implied exceeds George's to return any money borrowed as soon as David reaches Baltimore. George is then put to the test: if you send me money that will prove I still have "favour in your eyes"; fail me, though, and that will prove that "I am to be despised by (as I understand) a rich relation because when a *wild boy* I joined a profession which I then though and now think an honourable one. But which I would most willingly quite tomorrow if it gave satisfaction to your family provided I could do *any thing* else that would give bread to mine ..." Drunken blustering? A transparent attempt to rationalise a disastrous career decision? Or a sincere and desperate bid to provide for a growing family? The letter from George to William Clemm quoting cousin David's words is dated March 6 1809, so the incident and earlier letter described must have taken place and been written in the first few weeks of Edgar Poe's life. Things must have been desperate for the Poes. They got significantly worse the following year. David Poe had made his last stage appearance on October 18 1809 in New York City. Thereafter, he disappears entirely from the scene. In a letter of December 1835 to Judge Beverly Tucker, who had obviously seen Eliza on the stage, Poe refers to his parents having died "within a few weeks of each other". A document which purports to give the date and place of David's death as October 19 1810 in Norfolk, Virginia, is known to be a forgery, though one whose motivation is obscure. If David Poe had died in New York instead, no record would have been kept by the city. Only one circumstantial detail ties him to Norfolk. David stayed around long enough to impregnate Eliza for a third time and according to one version of events the luckless Rosalie was born at Norfolk on December 20 1810. Despite poor health – a letter of September 6 1812 states sadly that "poor little Rosalie is not expected to live" and makes reference to a hasty baptism – she was to be the only member of the immediate family to pass the age of 40. As it was she lived on until 1874, though her mind never developed beyond that of a child.

Such was Edgar Poe's family background. More than once over the years that followed he seemed inclined to disavow it by adopting an invented name – his most autobiographical story begins with the words "Let me call myself, *for the present*" – and the name by which he is known to history is the work of wishful thinking.

2

"Not a Spark of affection for us": Poe and his foster family, 1811–20

Elizabeth Arnold Hopkins Poe died on December 8 1811. Her eldest child and elder son, not yet five years old, was already being looked after by his grandfather. "General" Poe was not a wealthy man and was nearing 70 when his daughter in law passed away, but he could at least offer William Henry a stable and comfortable family life. However, even if David did not predecease her, Eliza died a *de facto* widow and there was no immediate provision for the younger Poe children.

In the event, they might be accounted lucky. As a baby, Rosalie would have shown no obvious sign of the arrested development that made her ironically long life a protracted infancy. Shortly after Eliza's death, she was taken in by a Mr and Mrs William Mackenzie of Richmond. By the same token, Edgar's later problems cannot confidently be attributed wholly to either nature or nurture. At the end of 1811, he was still a toddler, but with enough of his mother's vivid charm to catch the eye and warm the heart. There are various romantic versions of how Edgar might have first been noticed by the family whose name he assumed in addition to his own. It has been suggested that Eliza may in her daily walk to the theatre have carried the child, or pushed him in his baby carriage, past their house and business, but the geography is improbable and based on an anachronistic version of building dates. It is best to assume that in a town as small as Richmond was in the first decade of the 19th century – the United States Census Bureau gives the population as under 10,000 – a relatively successful actress and her child would be generally recognised, even if with a measure of suspicion by the more genteel.

By Christmas, Edgar was living with Mr and Mrs John Allan, or rather sharing the holidays with them at the Turkey Island home of planter Bowler Cocke. The Allans were childless and seemed to take delight in the boy. John's letters – the correspondence is large for the time and a valuable research resource – are peppered with references to Edgar, who seems to have gone through the usual childhood ailments, whooping cough and "the meazels", with less difficulty than his sister. There are also records of various expenses, for suits of clothes, a child's bed and, at the beginning of 1814, for schooling with a Miss Clotilda Fisher. He may have had other teachers, for a letter to Allan from a William Ewing also survives, enquiring about Edgar's further development and his reading. As Quinn notes in passing, it is unfortunate we do not have Allan's reply – he generally kept copies of correspondence – to the latter question. It would be fascinating to know what books the child was exposed to, though in the absence of a distinct children's literature at the time, one has to assume it would be a familiar mix of fairy tales, gods and mythological creatures, with perhaps a copy of John Newbery's *A Little Pretty Pocket-Book* (1744) often said to be the first non-didactic book written for children and sold, in a modern though hardly non-sexist touch, with a ball for boys or a pincushion for girls. Perhaps this is the "little Story Book" Edgar is described as holding; sadly, we have no definite information, but Allan, who was in England when Ewing wrote, was able to say that "Edgar is a fine Boy and I have no reason to complain of his progress".

The tone is interesting, as is the willingness to spend good money on the boy. Not least so, because it gives an impression of Allan's relations with Edgar that clashes strongly with their later dealings. John Allan is a key figure in Poe's life, but he is not well understood. Nor is their precise relationship. A number of sources suggest that the Allans adopted Edgar; a more accurate description would be that they fostered him. In the context of the times, with mortality high, childless or bereaved couples would sometimes take in orphaned relatives or illegitimate children of a lower social class, but while some such adoptions remained informal, there were legal mechanisms whereby Allan could have made Edgar his son. This he did not do, though school bills for Poe in London were made out in respect of "Masr. Allan". This might simply have been done for simplicity (maintaining an identity between pupil's name and the paying "parent"'s) or it may indicate that Allan was at this time happy to regard Edgar as his own. Back in Richmond five years later, similar bills were presented for the schooling of "Edgar Poe", but while one knows there were tensions in the family at this period – in addition to those inevitable in a household with a growing and vigorous boy – the reversion cannot in itself be adduced as a sign of cooling affections. From Poe's own part, his subsequent adoption of the name was in some measure an affectation and in further measure an understandable attempt to ingratiate himself with a man whose generosity seemed to flag as the foster-son moved towards adulthood and some hope of independence.

Much has been made of Edgar's adolescent and later correspondence with Allan, where in terms alarmingly similar to David Poe's angry, mawkish approach to George Clemm he begs his guardian for money. Read from the point of view that casts Poe as a drunken wastrel, these letters strongly tip the reader's sympathies towards Allan. In reality, when the student Poe complains that he has been given insufficient funds to support his studies, that seems to have been the case. According to one of Poe's early schoolmasters, the boy was "spoilt" with an excess of pocket money; the actual record shows something different, and there is no doubt that in later years, Allan deliberately kept him on short commons; the student Poe's desperate straits were not just a rationalisation of his own profligacy.

It is a puzzle, but then Allan is something of a puzzle. Literary history has tended to present him as rich and utterly pragmatic, generous but sensibly unwilling to indulge Poe's uncontrollable appetites. In reality, Allan was comfortably off but not wealthy, and while he was a punctilious businessman and an ambitious one, he seems to have had less about him of the dour Scotch bean-counter than prejudice suggests. Allan comes across in the letters as a bright and witty man of some education – the recognised quality of Scottish learning and literacy was the upside to the penny-pinching side of popular legend – and may even have nursed some ambitions to be a writer himself.

He was born in 1780 in the Ayrshire parish of Dundonald. The date is only confirmed by his tombstone, which declares that he died (March 27, 1834) in his 54th year. By the age of 15, Allan had emigrated to Virginia, where he joined an uncle, William Galt, who had come to the American colonies shortly before the Declaration of Independence. Travel, even correspondence, between Britain and the United States was slow and to some degree still perilous, but Allan seems to have been somewhat estranged from his family. He did not return to Scotland for twenty years and when he did visit in 1815, there seems to have been some degree of tension, perhaps a reflection of the widening economic and social divide between the prosperous American and his less sophisticated relatives; it is also worth underlining that for a period of time before the visit, their respective countries had been at war, and that the Napoleonic Wars had in addition put British agriculture and commerce under particular pressure.

After five years with his uncle's merchant's firm in Richmond, Allan and a fellow-clerk called William Ellis capitalised a new business which began trading in September 1801, dealing in tobacco and other commodities. The new concern seems to have been moderately successful, if not spectacularly so. Allan was a slave-holder, but he had this in common with most property-holding men of the time. He was not directly running a plantation, so presumably most of his slaves were used for warehouse work and stevedoring. If one looks for black marks against Allan, it might be possible to find one in his apparently casual instruction to sell one slave, a man called Scipio, for $600. However, the instruction came while Allan and his family were on shipboard, waiting in the Norfolk roads for a tide and a voyage to England that he privately believed would keep him away for at least five years.

If Edgar Allan Poe comes at the very beginning of American literature as a distinct entity, his foster-father or guardian was part of a first generation of American businessmen who did not represent a company back "home" in the United Kingdom but an American-owned concern. Allan was also one of the first to reverse the usual pattern in attempting to colonise the former coloniser by establishing a branch of Ellis & Allan in London, though again one has to wonder whether this was motivated entirely by business expansion or whether – and this is a tantalising thought, given Edgar's aesthetic values and loyalties – Allan hankered for the more sophisticated culture and pleasures of the Old World.

Richmond in 1800 was still a rough and ready town with still a hint of the frontier about it, though the period in question saw a significant wave of expansion and refurbishment, including new buildings in a Greek style somewhat influenced by Thomas Jefferson's architectural values. If the town was aspirational, so were the Allans. In February 1803, John married Frances Keeling Valentine of Princess Anne County, Virginia. On the basis of her letters, Fanny Allan was less academically educated than her husband (as would have been usual at the time) but seems to have had an artistic or at least aesthetic temperament, enjoying good furnishings and hangings in the house over the Ellis & Allan store at the junction of Main and Thirteenth Streets and holding regular entertainments there.

As was also relatively common at the time, Fanny's maiden sister lived with them, and there is every reason to suppose that little Edgar, "thin as a razor", was much indulged. The boy could only have had the dimmest memories of his birth mother, so Fanny did not so much replace her in Edgar's affections as create an idealised but slightly morbid image of motherhood which was projected backward onto the dead Eliza. Before Fanny died in 1829, Poe sent affectionate messages to her as "dearest Ma". Biographers have perhaps dwelt too much on the question of Poe's exact relations with John Allan, largely because there is a surviving correspondence. As so often in Poe's life, the most vexing questions often require only a small shift of perspective. He may never had a father's unqualified love, but he had two mothers, and their successive deaths did much to define and redefine him.

Edgar's infancy had been necessarily peripatetic and it seemed that circumstances were not going to allow him to settle for long into his comfortable Richmond home. On June 22 1815, the family set sail, arriving in Liverpool – presumably via the Azores – before the end of July. From now on, one looks for any experience that might feed directly into Poe's imagination. The voyage may not have been as hellish as those described in "MS Found in a Bottle", "Descent into the Maelstrom" or, indeed, *The Narrative of Arthur Gordon Pym*, but it seems to have been unpleasant, and Allan certainly later complained that the captain had been less than sympathetic. Who knows by how much relatively mild Atlantic storms and the seasickness suffered by Fanny and her sister were magnified in the mind of a six-year-old boy? Whatever the case, little Edgar wanted it to be known to William Ellis back in Richmond that he had been brave throughout the crossing and sent his love to "Rosa[lie]" and Mrs McKenzie. Allan affectionately added this in a postscript to his partner.

By the same token, and encouraged by the recognition that one of Poe's best stories, "William Wilson", is palpably autobiographical and rooted in his schooldays, one starts to look for any sign that arrival in the Old World – which would, indeed, seem old and atavistic to anyone raised in the young United States – and a subsequent trip to Scotland had struck some kind of Celtic chord in the boy's genetic make-up. The Allans' arrival coincided almost exactly with the beginnings of the still-anonymous Sir Walter Scott's cult reputation as "The Wizard of the North". Scott's first novel *Waverley,* published in 1814, began a world-wide mythologization of Scotland as a scene of heroic deeds, desperate ventures against alien authority (the Jacobite rising of 1745 would have resonated strongly with Americans who remembered the War of Independence), peopled by couthy speakers whose world-view was a curious combination of pragmatism and magic.

If Poe were influenced by Scott – and he certainly borrowed from him the terms "grotesque" and "arabesque", as well as the device of the orang-utan for "Murders in the Rue Morgue", which comes from Scott's *Count Robert of Paris* – the influence must have taken hold later, when Scott was a literary superstar and the unavoidable giant of world fiction. However, it may not be too far-fetched to say that the experience of reading Scott after having glimpsed some of those storied landscapes as a child may well have sharpened his appeal and impact. The crumbling houses, religious buildings and dark tarns around which Poe set many of his stories certainly weren't to be seen in or around Richmond and cannot be entirely dismissed as Gothic convention. A poem like "To the Lake" might be a memory of the visit or might be a further literary echo of Scott, the admired author of "The Lady of the Lake" before he became the enigmatic "Author of *Waverley*".

After Liverpool, Allan took the family north. They visited his sisters at Irvine, a small Ayrshire coastal town on the Firth of Clyde, not far from Allan's native Dundonald. A persistent legend suggests that Poe attended school here, but if he did, it can only have been for a matter of days and there is no evidence that he was sent back north to board. Allan made frequent business trips while the family stayed in Ayrshire, and seems to have made contacts in Greenock, Glasgow, Edinburgh, Newcastle and Sheffield, the last of these presumably en route to London. The family were established in the capital by the end of October 1815, living in lodgings on Southampton Row, to the east of Russell Square. The Allans occupied at least two addresses there, taking up more permanent residence at number 39.

John Allan had left Richmond in boom times and with high expectations. He was, however, not the first and would not be the last American whose return to the Old World was disillusioning. At the end of the Napoleonic Wars, the public debt was extensive, taxes were heavy and, combined with bad harvests, the country was in depression. George III, who had "lost the colonies", was still alive, but unfit to reign, and Britain was erratically stewarded by his son, the Prince Regent. The most glittering names of the Regency period – Beau Brummell, Jane Austen, Lord Byron, Sir Thomas Lawrence – and its high reputation for art and design offer only a partial picture of a country riven with faction and dissent; in one letter, Allan mentions that the Prince's carriage had been stoned.

The new firm of Allan & Ellis (the names reversed to reflect John's initiative in the enterprise) did not prosper as hoped. In addition, there were ongoing concerns about Frances Allan's health. She seems to have taken ill on the voyage across and never fully recovered. However, one wonders to what extent her malady was psychological, and if not contrived then exaggerated. It is clear that Fanny did not want to live in England. Allan confides in a letter that he had reassured her they would be away from Virginia for just three years, but telling his correspondent that five was a realistic minimum. Perhaps his wife took ill in hopes of being returned to Virginia (though she feared the sea) and stayed at Cheltenham for so long not so much in hope of any benefit from the waters as simply because Cheltenham was not grimy, dangerous London, and perhaps similar enough to Richmond to be consoling.

Whatever his difficulties, business and domestic, Allan did not stint on Edgar's care and education. The fact that he sent his foster son away to board should not be regarded as unduly significant. Edgar's English schooling began in Chelsea, too far for daily travel by a child, and in an establishment run by the Misses Dubourg, sisters of one of Allan's clerks. A century later, Poe scholar Killis Campbell uncovered the bills submitted to Allan by George Dubourg, who seems to have kept the school accounts in addition. It is touching to note that in addition to money for washing, catechisms and spelling books, and a seat in church, Alan paid an extra guinea a term so that Edgar did not have to share a bed with another boy. It isn't clear why Edgar was taken away from the Dubourg school. Perhaps he outgrew it, or showed sufficient promise to attend a more demanding establishment. Whatever the case, despite his flagging business hopes and undoubted concern for Fanny, Allan moved the boy to a more expensive school.

Poe's time at the Manor House School in Stoke Newington, then a village on the fringes of London, is important in that while earlier experiences and memories appear in his work only incidentally and verbally – the name Usher; No 39 Southampton Row, which appears in another, obscurer story; and the laundress Pauline Dubourg in "The Murders in the Rue Morgue" – his new headmaster, the Reverend John Bransby, appears as himself in what is arguably Poe's most autobiographical story, "William Wilson".

Bransby was clearly not flattered. Manor House itself, though, was flattered considerably in its physical aspects at least by Poe's description. "William Wilson" may be autobiographical, but it is not without embellishment, and the plain functional Manor House was for a long time confused with the more elaborate "Laurels" which stood opposite and from which Poe took some of his detail. Poe did in one small detail add to Bransby's stature by referring to him as "Dr". Even without a doctorate, the headmaster was an impressive one by the standards of the time, a fine classical scholar and student of botany, who combined clerical authority – he was also minister of the church the boys attended twice each Sunday – with an enthusiasm for sport and a belief in what became the Victorian principle of *mens sana in corpore sano*.

Like all boys, Poe perhaps exaggerated Bransby's solemnity and discipline. Like all writers, he turned the real space of Manor House into a metaphor for the mind and the imagination, a limitless, mazy location in which to lose oneself. "William Wilson" was written and published two decades after the time it evokes, but it does seem to memorialise the beginnings of Poe's conscious life and of his vocation as a writer. It is a story about a boy whose conscience is so excessively developed that it is reified as a second, living self. One hardly needs to have read Freud or to understanding the function of the superego to detect in this the anguish of a man who believed himself abandoned by two fathers in turn.

∞∞∞∞

John Allan was perhaps more distracted by his own problems than neglectful. By the autumn of 1819, he was writing to Charles Ellis in some despair, complaining of being down to his last £100 and unable even to travel back to the US without some financial assistance. The London firm was wound up, apparently with all debts settled, and on June 8 1820, delayed only slightly by the arrival back in Britain of Queen Caroline, the Allans and Edgar set sail for New York on the *Martha*.

The Queen's brave return, to face charges of adultery and possibly treason laid by her estranged husband, was perhaps a further reminder of the political and financial chaos Allan was escaping. Caroline of Brunswick (in a rare slip, Quinn identifies her as "Charlotte", the wife of the late George III, who herself had died two years previously) was bent on attending George IV's coronation; he was equally determined to stop her. She took ill on the very day he was crowned, and died insisting she had been poisoned. One senses John Allan's relief to be going.

Writing to Ellis from the quayside he proclaims "I for myself never was better". He was, however, considerably dependent on his partner. When the family arrived back in Richmond, they lived with the Ellises for nearly a year before moving into a house provided for them by William Galt. Edgar seems to have struck up a friendship with young Thomas Ellis and with some other boys, including Robert Sully, whose father had acted with Eliza Poe. This may have afforded the boy some vicarious contact with his dead mother, but it also served as a reminder of his lowly origins and there seems to have been a certain amount of snobbish disdain directed at Poe in aristocratic Richmond, mostly by his schoolmates, but very probably on the word of their parents.

Interestingly and perhaps significantly, he was "Edgar Poe" again and not "Master Allan". Whether this implies some cooling of John's affection can only be speculation, but it certainly would have pointed up the boy's schoolyard visibility as a dependent orphan. After the failure of the London venture, Allan was in difficulties. In 1822, he seems to have made some kind of personal insolvency arrangement; two years later, the partnership with Ellis was dissolved. However, there was money to be made in a state rich in valuable commodities, and with his undoubted head for business, Allan clawed his way back to prosperity. Even during the bleakest times, he continued to pay for Edgar's education, even if he subconsciously grudged such an expense at such a time for a child not his own. There was another factor. Poe was a child no longer. Adolescence brings with it many tensions and a familiar roster of complaints. In the summer of 1824, Allan replied on Edgar's behalf to a letter from Henry Poe, furious that Edgar should have failed to acknowledge his brother. In its final pages, the letter takes an odd turn into pious, almost mawkish language, advising Henry, whose precise problems at this time are not known, to place his trust in God and prayer, but its opening description of the teenage Edgar is almost stereotypical: "he does nothing", "miserable", "sulky", "ill-tempered", "not a Spark of affection for us not a particle of gratitude for all my care and kindness toward him", and much else in that vein. Allan's apparent respect and affection for Henry is intriguing, given how shadowy a figure the older Poe boy remains, and the contrast between him and Edgar, and between the ingrate, unfeeling Edgar and "poor Rosalie" is drawn very sharply indeed. Allan makes it clear that this change in behaviour dates from the family's return to Richmond: "a line of thinking & acting very contrary to what he possessed in England".

At the Manor House in Stoke Newington, Edgar had obviously made good progress; his reading, writing and Latin seem to have been quite advanced, and it is probable that, while only "dancing" is mentioned on Bransby's school bill as an extra cost, he took part in sports as well. Those who knew Poe in childhood remember him as boisterous, given to reckless adventure – he claimed to have swum the James River five miles against the tide in the heat of a summer day – and quick with his fists. Whether this was attention-seeking by a lonely boy, or a natural defence against bullying, or whether it was the self-conscious physicality adopted by very clever boys so as not to appear too bookish and accommodating is merely another object of conjecture. However, it serves to dispel any tendency to see Poe, at any stage in his life except the last, as morose and neurasthenic, with a revulsion from physical activity; that, again, is to confuse him with his characters.

Hindsight is doubly dangerous when applied to a character of Poe's already controversial reputation, but the most realistic picture that emerges of him and of his relationship with his foster-father is scarcely unusual and in few respects deeply troubling. Edgar Poe seems to have been an active, sociable youth, quick at his lessons, and keen to lead astray if he was not allowed to lead. A foretaste of the effective soldier he was to become can be had from his time as Lieutenant Edgar A. Poe (he was already using that form of name) in the Junior Volunteers, a youthful militia who may have served as an informal honour guard when "General" Poe's old friend the Marquis de Lafayette visited Virginia later that year. On the external evidence, Poe was not as idle or undisciplined as Allan complained. Gratitude and affection are famously difficult to measure and "misery" is very subjective indeed.

There is another factor, and another possible explanation, for Poe's moods and John Allan's reaction. His own moral standards seemed to have eroded since the return from England. Allan was unfaithful to Frances and whether Edgar knew this in any explicit detail – Richmond was a small town and it is remarkable what boys pick up in playground talk and on back-alley sorties – he might well have detected Fanny's unhappiness. By the same token, guilty men often exaggerate their criticism of others' moral failings as a kind of smokescreen for their own.

Poe certainly didn't strike other adults as disagreeable. Around this time, he met Mrs Jane Craig Stanard, a beautiful Richmond lady and the mother of a friend. She seems to have taken the boy seriously and shown him affection. Poe seems to have visited her when things were difficult at home. With a perverse inevitability, though, Mrs Stanard was just the next adored woman and mother-surrogate to come into Poe's life only to leave it abruptly. Following a period of illness marked by some form of mania or dementia, she died in the spring of 1824. It is not clear whether Edgar saw her while she was mad, an experience which would have had a powerful, possibly traumatic effect, but there is a story that for a period after her death he paid nightly visits to her grave.

It had been, of course, a platonic relationship, further sublimated in one of his most beautiful and formally perfect lyrics, "To Helen", which Poe liked to suggest had been written at the time, though it was not published until 1831. As with any fifteen-year-old boy, though, Edgar's hormones were raging. Having experienced an idealised love for an older woman, he then fell in love for real.

There is, as ever in this story, some uncertainty as to how and where Poe met Elmira Royster and whether the "enchanted garden" in which they carried on their courtship was anything more than a romantic figment. Elmira's claim to have been a near-neighbour of the Allans does not square with the existing record; Poe scholars have been fanatically scrupulous in tracing the social geography of Richmond at the time. Their courtship and an apparent engagement continued for some time, and Poe continued to write to the girl after he left to study at the University of Virginia. Unfortunately, the correspondence was intercepted by Elmira's father, who refused the young couple permission to marry.

Given the received view of Poe, it might be tempting to imagine Mr Royster barring his daughter's door against the wild importunings of a dangerous Heathcliffian poet, who perhaps also smelled of brandy. It seems, though, that Royster simply thought they were to young to wed – this was Elmira's belief in later life – though his insistence may have reflected a concern that Poe had not yet a settled career and may have been further compounded by a shiver of snobbish distaste at the thought of his daughter marrying the son of strolling players. There seems to have been nothing else at the time that would have caused him concern. Speaking in 1875 to the archivist Edward V. Valentine, Mrs Sarah Elmira Royster Shelton remembered Poe with great warmth as quiet and chivalrous, "beautiful" but with a hint of melancholy. She emphatically confirms that her father's objections were to do with their age – "no other reason" – and describes her sadness when anything "scurrilous" is said about Poe, a pointed comment at any point in that quarter-century after his death when the reputation was at its lowest and the "Griswold version" of the life the basis of consensus. There is another interesting remark, again delivered plainly enough to carry conviction. Unlike the procession of would-be Helens who claimed that Poe had addressed verses to them, Elmira did not recall any such thing during their romance: no love-sonnets, no apostrophes to the Muse.

So: at eighteen, Poe was turning into manhood conscious of his precarious position in the world, or at least in Richmond society. He had known some sadness, some loss, some adventure, some conflict, and had at least tasted love in its adult form. He was neither wild nor dissolute, nor yet, in any public way at least, a poet.

"The most dissolute university of Europe": Poe and further education, 1820–29

Though they grew up in different households, Rosalie Poe seems to have held Edgar in special affection, devotedly following him around Richmond, perhaps an unwelcome "third wheel" when he tried to steal time with Elmira. By contrast, and for all John Allan's bizarrely misplaced admiration, Henry Poe scarcely registers at all. There was, however, a meeting between the brothers in 1825, during which Henry apparently confided his dreams of foreign travel. Poe himself frequently spoke in later years as if he had taken part in Byronic adventures in Greece (where he claimed to have fought for her independence) and Russia, or sought enlistment in the Polish army, or to have travelled in South America, but these were imaginary or wishful projections, some perhaps taken second-hand from his brother. After returning from England with his foster-parents, Edgar Allan Poe never again left the continental United States, but his imagination, already fuelled by reading, seems to have been set on fire by Henry's pipedreams, and the poetry that would begin to emerge from

Poe's pen over the next few years was cast in exotic languages and set in romantic, or "arabesque" locations.

His physical – and intellectual – horizons did broaden that year, but Poe's university career was destined to be short. It is a strange and disturbing episode that marks a steadily worsening relationship with John Allan, whose behaviour at this period is so odd that it almost certainly camouflages some crisis of a personal nature.

Poe matriculated at the University of Virginia, Charlottesville, on February 14 1826, and signed up to take courses in ancient and modern languages with George Long, the youthful but brilliant professor of classics, and with George Blaetterman, an irascible German who was famed less for his scholarship than for the notorious occasion when he horsewhipped his wife in the street. Poe's lodgings were at No 13 (of course!) West Range, part of the classically-inspired campus founded by Thomas Jefferson and dominated by the Rotunda, which was modelled on the Pantheon.

The university had only opened the year before and was an innovation – some contemporaries would have said anomaly or even aberration – in American education. It was, for a start, strictly non-denominational and, as part of Jefferson's mission to breed a new generation of thinking democrats, was student-run, with no executive principal or president. Pastoral care was left in the hands of the so-called "hotel-keepers" who looked after the lodgings. Jefferson visited and dined with the students whenever occasion allowed; Poe makes no mention of a meeting, though it is probable that he saw the founder at some point.

It sounds idyllic, even utopian, but the University of Virginia rapidly acquired a bad reputation for drunkenness, gambling and brawls. Two of Poe's letters home to Richmond refer to "disturbances in College" and "a great many fights" (one of which is graphically described), and he mentions that shortly after Allan took him up to Charlottesville, the Grand Jury and sheriffs had been called in. The failure of self-governance brought about a backlash and faculty were given stringent powers which, in turn and inevitably, led to more unrest among the student body.

In "William Wilson", where the phrase "the Draconian laws of the academy" is applied to Bransby's school rather than university, the hero moves on to Eton and Oxford and sinks ever deeper into dissolution, addicted to wine and cards. Early biographers were inclined to cherry-pick auto-biographical elements from the story as occasion or need demanded, but it was always assumed that Poe's Oxford – "the most dissolute university of Europe" was simply an imaginative projection, an example long before Henry James codified the transatlantic theme of the innocent New World looking on in horror at the decadence of the Old. "William Wilson" may in fact offer a reasonably accurate picture of life at Charlottesville, though not necessarily of Poe's own behaviour. He may not have been surrounded by the "haughtiest heirs of the wealthiest earldoms in Great Britain", but the aristocratic young Virginians he mingled at Charlottesville were certainly the North American equivalent and no less dissipated for being scions of a younger nation. Matters grew so bad on campus that fifteen years after Poe's time there, a distinguished professor was murdered while trying to stop a riot.

Poe seems to have thrived academically. He is mentioned with distinction for his work in French and with credit for Latin. Though he made limited use of the library, which operated according to a cumbersome system of written permissions to borrow, his reading seems relatively ambitious and obviously confident in French. He joined the Jefferson Debating Society and served on its committee. The one-time Richmond Junior Volunteer may have joined the university cadet corps; given that he thrived in uniform and enjoyed command, it would be odd had he not.

This picture of a "model student" calls for some humanising touches. Poe's friend Miles George, sometimes incorrectly identified as a room-mate, is no help at first, dismissing their much-discussed fist-fight as a "boyish freak or frolic", begun over something trivial and forgotten by mutual consent. He presents Poe as gifted in "quoting poetic authors and reading poetic productions of his own" (a further indication that the young man was not just experimenting in verse, but doing so publicly) and an accomplished sketch artist, who could at a whim produce whimsical caricatures on a dormitory wall. Only then does George sound a darker note, suggesting that Poe could be melancholic as well as frolicsome and – at last! – that he had a vice. "To calm & quiet the excessive nervous excitability under which he laboured, he would too often put himself under the influence of that 'Invisible Spirit of Wine' which the great dramatist has said 'If known by no other name should be called Devil'-".

There is a giveaway tone here. One hears it in the sorrowful tut-tut of "too often" and the recourse to literary authority. George solemnly grips his lapels and addresses posterity. His memories were written down in 1880, by which time the posthumous image of Poe as a dissolute drunk was well established. One can surely indulge George in a desire to have us know that he was among the first to spot and regret what was to become so tragically obvious later. Ladies imagined Poe had addressed love poems to them; men insisted they had taken too much wine with him. This is how one claims a small stake in greatness. But, just as his squabbles with Allan might be dismissed as natural adjuncts to adolescence, was Poe's drinking at this age anything out of the ordinary for a university student? Does it suggest high spirits or depression? What was he really trying to suppress?

There is clear evidence that a rift had opened up between Poe and his foster-father. It probably has a deeper subtext, and a distasteful one, but unlike the complaints made in Allan's letter to Henry, the bases of this conflict are clearly quantifiable. In other circumstances, Allan would have had every reason to feel satisfaction at his foster-son's progress, but one wonders at his motives in sending Edgar to university in the first place and the sabotaging way it was done. There is a letter to Allan, written some three years after the events described, in which Edgar's sense of injustice sharpens a very convincing recall of detail. Poe states that while a term of study at university cost $350, Allan only provided him with $110, and then abused him for only attending two courses rather than the requisite three when the boy's allowance would not stretch to paying the mathematics professor. One detects a familiar pang when Poe describes the stigma of poverty and ostracism from better company. The letter makes a familiar turn into self-pity, saying that he fell into bad ways "because it was my crime to have no one on Earth who cared for me, or loved me", but also a sense of lonely desperation.

Why did Allan keep Poe short? Why send him away at all if he resented the expense? Perhaps "away" is the operative word. If, as seems likely from subsequent correspondence, Poe had expressed gallant disapproval of Allan's unfaithfulness, he may simply have wanted rid of a boy who threatened him with exposure. Charlottesville was not far away, but would have been far enough. As ever, the facts are muddied by contradictory evidence and interpretation. Instead of giving Edgar money to pay for a college uniform, Allan had one made and sent: meanness, or good Scotch common-sense? One can understand that if Allan did later undertake to pay some of Edgar's debts, he might well refuse to pay those that resulted from gambling. It does seem, though, that despite the testimony of Ellis's son, John actually refused to pay some outstanding bills, for clothes and for a college servant. In that same letter, Edgar insisted that his habits were regular and far from dissolute, that he took to gambling only as a last-ditch attempt to keep afloat but then had to borrow heavily from the "Jews in Charlottesville at extravagant interest".

One shouldn't rely on figures simply because they are figures. In a sarcastic reference to his time at Charlottesville – too short, he reminds Allan, to acquire a "liberal education" – Poe refers to spending "8 months at the University of Va" when it was actually ten, but he also underestimates the real cost of a term of study, so no hair is being split. Poe's gaming debts have been estimated as between $2000 and $2500; no mean sum, though the issue at point is not so much the actual figure as how these and other debts were handled. Again many years after the events in question, Thomas Ellis suggested that John Allan had come up to Charlottesville and settled all bills except those that resulted from gambling. Unfortunately, the documentary evidence conflicts. Allan was still being pursued two years later for relatively small amounts owed by "Mr Pow" to a haberdasher and for the use of a college servant. By this point, Allan seems to have all but washed his hands of Poe.

Again with long hindsight, Ellis remembered that Allan brought Poe back to Richmond and set him to work in the accounting department of Ellis & Allan, which must at the turn of 1826/1827 have been in the late stages of winding-up.

This also appears to conflict with a letter from Poe to Allan written some three months after his removal from the University of Virginia in which he says: "You have moreover ordered me to quit your house, and are continually upbraiding me with eating the bread of idleness, when you yourself were the only person to remedy the evil by placing me to some business-". This is potentially ambiguous, but appears to say that Allan was the only person *in a position to* remedy the evil, rather than that he had done so. Further correspondence makes the matter clear. Poe looked to Allan for work; none was forthcoming.

He would continue to plead for assistance from "My dear Pa" and may even have received small sums from Frances Allan and her sister Anne – or "Nancy" – Valentine, but relations had for the moment broken down catastrophically. Though circumstances would bring him back to the South sooner than he might have wanted, on or around March 24 1827, Poe left Richmond for good. Before the year was out, he would become an enlisted soldier and a published poet.

∞∞∞∞

Poe showed little overt affection for his birthplace in later years, but it was to Boston that he gravitated in that first spring of his precarious independence, perhaps because it was a place associated with his mother, more probably because it offered more to an aspiring writer than Virginia possibly could. His first collection *Tamerlane and Other Poems*, published that summer, was headed "By a Bostonian". No sign that Poe made further use of the pseudonym "Henri Le Rennet" which is mentioned at one point by Allan, and which may have been a combination of angry affectation and incipient breakdown, but also more practically a useful way of shaking creditors off his scent. When he enlisted, he signed on as "Edgar A. Perry", which interestingly rejects the Poe half of his surname and preserves the Allan.

Soldier, poet, office clerk (which is how he gave his occupation on an enlistment form) ... but an actor as well? Did Poe follow his parents onto the Boston stage? Thomas Ellis claimed he had, but in 1941 Arthur Hobson Quinn could find only one possible reference, a newspaper advertisement for a production of *Foundling of the Forest,* in which "the part of Bertrand by a young gentleman of Boston, his first appearance on any stage, who has politely proffered his services on the occasion". Poe had enjoyed domestic theatricals in Richmond, so the teasing possibility remains.

He must, in any case, have had the poems for *Tamerlane* in his pocket when he went up to Boston. His claim that some of these were written in his fourteenth year is scarcely credible, and may serve as nothing more than self-conscious recognition by one for whom verse is "not a purpose, but a passion" that they are not as good as the young poet would want them to be. In fact, they are very good indeed, worked and reworked with a passionate purposefulness, and for all the apparent Byronic influence, already very individual. The title poem exists in various manuscript versions and was republished two years later in revised form, and then again with further changes in 1831. The epigraph to the first edition prepares the way for this. It comes from William Cowper: "Young heads are giddy and young hearts are warm / And make mistakes for manhood to reform."

This, in itself, marks it out as something important in Poe's body of work, for "Tamerlane" not only sketches in his great themes for the first time – the pride of the exceptional individual set over against the "rabble-men", beauty as an absolute, passion as an aesthetic position, the imminence/immanence of death – and establishes the Poe voice in its distinctive metrics and tolling cadences. It also introduces a writer who is all about careful *re*invention, an important line of concern in English verse all the way from Metaphysicals like John Donne and most particularly, George Herbert, to Robert Browning and the modernists. We overstate the case in insisting that Poe considered his short lyrics to be verbal icons, as complete and irreducible in intention and effect as porcelain. Right from the beginning – and this is what makes him seem modern – Poe is always conscious, and always makes us conscious of the text as text and of the writer's role in shaping it. This became a device when he turned to writing prose fiction and often used the device of the "found" document.

Poe instinctively adopted the four-stress line as the closest to natural speech. The dying Tamerlane addresses a priest but in the very first lines rejects any need for "kind solace". Here and subsequently, the old man acts as a negative foil and a dramatic intermediary; Tamerlane neither soliloquises nor addresses the reader. "Know thou the secret of a spirit / Bow'd from its wild pride into shame." "I was ambitious – have you known / The passion, father? You have not ..." There is defiance in this, and the arrogance of someone who knows that his listener could not have shared in his passions, but there is also pathos – "I have not always been as now" – and Poe shows a remarkable gift for conveying emotion, anger, pain even, by varying his metre. With "You call it hope – that fire of fire! / It is but agony of desire ..." one might say that the stress-pattern wavers in the second half of the couplet. That is precisely the point: the line enacts its meaning.

It is a long poem by a poet who later insisted that such a thing was a contradiction in terms. Significantly, later revisions left it much shorter. The remaining poems in the collection – "The Lake", "Imitation", "To ------" (probably Elmira), "Evening Star", "Visit of the Dead", "Dreams" – are all brief lyrics, more interesting as an early insight into Poe's reigning obsessions than as prosody. They are, however, more revealing of the young poet at work than some of the later, more perfect poems. Some were later reprinted, some revised, like "Tamerlane" itself, some abandoned, but always with a shrewd critical logic. Poe's analytical treatise, "The Rationale of Verse" was only published in the *Southern Literary Messenger* a matter of months before his death but it represents a lifetime of thinking on the subject. Not until Ezra Pound was there an American poet with a more acute ear.

Tamerlane and Other Poems was published in the summer of 1827 by the young Boston printer Calvin F. S. Thomas, who was about a year older than Poe. Unfortunately, Thomas left no recollection of their association. Poe's age was a moot point; he gave it as 22 when he enlisted. This might seem a pointless distortion since, as Quinn makes clear, the United States army did at the time accept under-age cadets. It is possible that the 18-year-old Poe might have believed he would need a parent's or guardian's written permission to sign up and was anxious to prevent Allan learning his whereabouts or intentions. Poe did later write to Allan asking permission to leave the army, though that might simply have been an attempt to ingratiate. He also seems to have told a later commanding officer that his parents had been victims of the Richmond theatre fire.

He made no other obvious attempt to cover his tracks. If the 22 year old "Perry" was an invention, there seems less reason to doubt the other details given on his enlistment papers: eyes – grey, hair – brown, complexion – fair, occupation – clerk.

Perhaps he was measured, or perhaps he added an inch or so when he gave his height as 5'8", a respectable stature for the age. Either way, it is the first objective physical description we have of the young man who was trying so hard *not* to be Edgar Allan Poe.

Fate, in the shape of military orders, quickly obliterated the distance he had put between himself and Virginia. Poe was initially assigned to Battery H of the First Artillery, at Fort Independence in Boston Harbour but was shortly thereafter posted to Fort Moultrie, on Sullivan's Island in Charleston Harbour. He was there long enough for the place – dunes, scrub, low myrtles, shells – to sink into his imagination; it emerges in "The Gold Bug", an early story whose hero Legrand has settled on the island, "a very singular one. It consists of little else than the sea sand and is about three miles long. Its breadth at no point exceeds a quarter of a mile. It is separated from the mainland by a scarcely perceptible creek, oozing its way through a wilderness of reeds and slime".

Poe's time under uniform is often dismissed as brief, but peacetime soldiering can be wearisome and the posting to Moultrie would have seemed interminable to Poe. He was there from mid-November 1827 to December 1828, when he was transferred to Fort Monroe in Virginia. There would have been plenty time to quarter the claustrophobic island in off-duty hours, and the plot of "The Gold Bug" is exactly the kind of elaborate puzzle-mystery one might concoct in such a place.

Though time weighed heavy on him, Poe seems to have been an able enough soldier, recognised by his officers – one of whom was called Griswold, a name that will resonate ironically later, though the individual is unrelated – and trusted at his work. His discharge papers speak of him as efficient, praiseworthy, "free from bad habits", "free from drinking"; qualities that had led, on January 1 1829, to Poe being promoted from artificer to sergeant-major. It is not unknown for promotion to heighten discontent rather than salve it. A man who has served many years as a private soldier without overt complaint may suddenly chafe as soon as he is rewarded with rank. So it was with Poe. He started to think in terms of leaving the army and enrolling as a cadet at West Point, which had been established in 1802 as the United States military academy, occupying a large site fifty miles north of New York City.

Poe required – or wanted – Allan's consent for such a move and needed his sponsorship as well. There had been an exchange of letters during Poe's service at Moultrie. They seem affectionate enough, expressing concern for Allan's health, some remorse for his own behaviour at Charlottesville and his "wayward disposition"; the prodigal, if such he was, seems inclined to repent amends. There is a discord, then, when one turns to a letter of recommendation Allan wrote for Edgar in May 1829, a little over a month after his army discharge. Allan excuses his frankness of tone "but I address a soldier" – Major John H. Eaton was secretary of war – and states with extraordinary detachment that Poe, who had been addressing Allan in letters as "father" and "my dear Pa" has never stood any differently in his affections than any other poor soul in distress; "Frankly, Sir, do I declare that he is no relation to me whatever ..." True to the letter, but an odd sort of recommendation, particularly when it also lists Poe's gambling problems and debts as a student. Allan does at least mention that Edgar performed well in his schools at the end of the year. It seems that Allan gave out the impression elsewhere that Edgar had absconded from university and had not been in contact for "some years". By the same token, Poe made it known that Allan was rarely sober.

It is again hard to know what to make of this, beyond an increasingly rancorous relationship. There were, however, two possible factors in play. How one decides between them rather depends on previous impressions of Allan's character, and possibly also of Poe's behaviour. Frances Allan's death on the last day of February 1829 may have removed a final check on Allan's growing impatience with his foster-son. Poe was not present at the funeral, but does seem to have arrived in Richmond on leave the following day and there is a surviving order for a suit of mourning clothes, paid for by Allan. Its very survival is a further sign of how punctilious Allan was in all matters of business, however small and under whatever circumstances, so it must have enraged him when, not much more than a month later, Edgar seemed once again to have violated his strict code of conduct in financial matters. It was the practice at the time for soldiers leaving the army to buy themselves out by paying for a substitute. This usually involved a small fee made out to the commanding officer who would simply administer the replacement of a retiring man with the next mustered recruit. Unfortunately, Poe's colonel was not on base at the beginning of April, so Poe seems to have struck a private arrangement with a Sergeant Samuel Graves for very much more than the usual sum, paying some of the amount in cash and offering a note for the rest, meanwhile pocketing some of the money Allan had sent for precisely this transaction. Poe's dealings with Graves are, as ever, clouded in contradiction, and it may be that the debt they later disputed was actually for money borrowed rather than the substitution. Either way, the irregularity would have infuriated Allan.

This is the same man who made provision in his will for twin sons that a certain Mrs Elizabeth Wills "says are mine, I do not know their names"; provision was also made for a daughter. Allan's probity in business was not always matched in private life, and even allowing for different standards of behaviour at the time and for the strong probability that Frances Allan's poor health meant their relationship had not been a physical one for some years, it is hard to believe that his grief at her death was long, deep or even genuine. In October 1830 Allan was remarried to a Louisa Gabriella Patterson of Elizabethtown, New Jersey. He makes clear in a rider to his will that his affair with Mrs Wills was over before he met his new wife but that he had made a clean breast of the relationship; typically, he makes no reference to whether Frances had known. Allan's second marriage was not childless. The arrival of three sons – John Jr in August 1831, William in October 1832 and Patterson in January 1834, just weeks before his father's death – was a source of both pride and some social and financial embarrassment (since he already had to provide for illegitimate children). One wonders what effect it subsequently had on Poe, who could be forgiven for thinking that his marginalisation was complete. A mother had different loyalties to a foster-mother, and Louisa Allen had no emotional history with Edgar, whom she met as an adult. There can be no doubt that she played an active part in putting him aside.

In the meantime, with all this some way in the future, and despite the tensions, Poe continued to regard Richmond as his home. When he left there at the end of May to head north for West Point examinations and commencements, Allan must have been preoccupied with the later stages of Mrs Wills' double pregnancy, and Poe would surely have been aware of that. Yet he remained dependent on Allan, not just finan-cially but also emotionally. It is possible that leaving a family situation where one has felt less than secure, even rejected, is harder than taking wing from something more securely loving. Ironically, Allan's second marriage took place in New York, bringing him close to Edgar once more, just another switched polarity in the curious pattern of attraction and repulsion, brusque rejection and seemingly genuine affection, recrimination and dependence that marked their relationship.

Poe remembered that when they parted on the quayside he had the strongest feeling that they would not see each other again. The two men continued to orbit uneasily until Allan's death in 1834, or rather Poe orbited him, a small, erratic sat-ellite on a desperate elliptical path, never sure whether what lay beneath him was hospitable and kindly or flinty and cold. For all his deep ambivalence towards Allan, for all his genuine complaints and vicious untruths (like those about Allan's drinking), and for all his flagrantly attention-seeking behav-iour, Poe, who had already lost three mothers or mother-fig-ures, had known no other father.

4

"A dream within a dream": Poe's early work, 1829–31

"No Cadet shall keep in his room any novel, poem or other book, not relating to his studies, without permission from the superintendent." It is a stricture that would perturb even an averagely voracious reader but must have been agonising to a published poet who believed he had the mark of genius upon him. Whatever motivated his return to the military – desperation cannot be ruled out but nor can a wish for social advancement as a member of the officer class – Poe quickly recognized that military discipline was incompatible with his romantic temperament and his ambitions as a writer. He spent just eight months as a West Point cadet before being dishonourably discharged.

Though there was an air of inevitability to his departure, Poe had to contrive a clash with authority. Just as in the artillery, he seems to have been an excellent student but was increasingly settled in a literary vocation. His second and third volumes of verse, revised and extended versions of his first, with new poems and the first prose inklings of Poe's aesthetic theories, were published in December 1829 and in April or May 1831.

The latter was dedicated to "The U.S. Corps of Cadets".

Poe was no longer a cadet himself when it appeared, and the reason for the dedication was pragmatic, as will be seen. He had enrolled at West Point in June 1830, taking the entrance examination – basically a literacy and numeracy test – with ease. He was billeted at 28 South Barracks, a room he shared with a Thomas W. Gibson and a Timothy Pickering Jones, both of whom much later, at the turn of the 20th century, offered accounts of Poe as they "remembered" him. Predictably, their memories are contradictory; equally predictably, they involve heavy surreptitious drinking at a nearby shebeen. Some elements of their recollections ring consonantly and true. Poe was charming but melancholy, and a gifted satirist. There is no need to consider their recall of his scholastic performance since the official record survives. Poe came 17th out of 87 in his mathematics class (this, remember, the subject he was not able to pick up at Charlottesville; a contemporary recalled he was "too mad a poet to like Mathematics"), but came third in French. The remainder of his time, and indeed the whole of the first two months of his cadetship, was taken up with military exercises and drills. If Poe was academically ahead of most of his fellows, he would also have been familiar with basic soldiering and there is no reason to think that he fell short in any way.

Simply, his dreams rested elsewhere. Between his discharge from the army and his enrolment at West Point, Poe spent a period of time in Baltimore, visiting family connections and meeting Marylanders who had known his grandfather. He also made contact with his aunt Maria Clemm, the daughter of David Poe Sr and widow of William Clemm Jr, whose first wife had been Maria's cousin Harriet Poe. Maria looms large and ambiguously later in Poe's life and it was her daughter

Virginia, just seven years old in 1829, who six years later became Poe's notorious child-wife. Poe does not seem to have lodged with the Clemms at this period, but Maria may have helped him out with money.

His sources of income at this period remain obscure. Poe was hawking around a new collection. He took his growing bundle of poems to Philadelphia where it was shown to publishers Carey, Lea & Carey, a prestigious imprint. Poe wrote back to Richmond suggesting that the firm might well take on the little book if Allan would agree to underwrite any loss which he believed would not exceed $100 even if not a single copy were sold. He adds that "I have long given up Byron as a model" – whether moral or poetical he does not say – "for which, I think, I deserve some credit". In the now familiar pattern, Allan, who was still paying Poe's out of pocket expenses, brusquely refused, in his own words "strongly censuring [Edgar's] conduct". The "Bully Graves" affair still rumbled on in the background and there were probably other black marks or perceived wrongdoings against Poe's name, but it is tempting to wonder whether literary envy kept Allan's pursestrings knotted; he had, after all, entertained some notion of becoming a writer himself. In a different letter, he mocked Poe's constant importunings, saying that no great artist had ever relied on charity.

The main poem that Poe was showing at this time was "Al Aaraaf", a curious and still seriously underrated work in which Poe takes a great step forward in his desire to fuse meaning with a distinctive verbal music that worked at a level beyond semantics. The poem is obscure, oddly tangled in logic, and riven with baffling transitions, but it is by no means juvenilia.

The title refers to the supernova discovered in 1572 in the

constellation Cassiopeia by the astronomer Tycho Brahe, who regarded its appearance and disappearance as an ill omen. The title is a corruption of the Arabic *Al Orf*, or more strictly its plural form, and this in turn is derived from a word whose meanings include schism or polarisation. For Poe, this realm of ill omen is a version of Limbo or perhaps Purgatory (though he takes something here, and in "Israfel" later from the Koran, he also subsequently flirted with Catholic imagery in "Morella", specifically the "Hymn" section, and in "To Mary") where the souls are simply denied the appreciation of beauty. This is the poem's keynote. The figure of Nesace represents the quintessence and sanctity of beauty whose mission to the spheres is a version of the Keatsian identification of beauty and truth. The poem is imbued with Poe's characteristically heterodox version of "as above, so below", a principle that underpinned the thinking of the Puritans and Transcendentalists with the idea that events on earth and the moral principles guiding them were simply a microcosm of what governed the universe. Poe's version is more radical, suggesting a deceptive congruence between the cosmic and the particular and hinting that the "'Idea of Beauty'" (for Poe the defining human invention) might not so much transform as actually corrupt if it is not accompanied by some commitment to the truth. The poem is full of yearning distances, states of being that dissolve into evanescence, and vast swoops back and forth between the personal and the universal, but it also strikingly lacks that sense of an excluded ethical middle between those two states detected by the New Humanist critic Irving Babbitt in his 1919 demolition of Rousseau's brand of Romanticism. Though Poe at first glance seems to suspend any condition between the merely sensory or aesthetic and the eternal, his very self-consciousness regarding these polarities brings them every time back into the realm of the human.

Some of "Al Aaraaf" is very high-flown indeed. As Nesace kneels among the earthly/unearthly flowers, Poe offers a breathless taxonomy that climaxes with this:

And Valisnerian lotus, thither flown
From struggling with the waters of the Rhone:
And thy most lovely perfume, Zante!
Isola d'oro – Fior de Levante!

These are verses (they reappear later in "Sonnet – to Zante") that seem to look back to the "Oriental romance" of the Irish poet Thomas Moore's *Lalla Rookh* (1817) and forward to the strange, polycultural macaronics of Ezra Pound's *The Cantos*. Pound always insisted that rhythm was the essential component of a distinctive poet voice, its only reliable giveaway.

Poe's embrace of irrationality and objectless passion as higher expressions of human endeavour than reason and empiricism might lead to an assumption that he was ignorant of contemporary science. Such a view is easily confounded by reference to *Eureka,* the long, strange essay of 1848 (which Poe chose to regard as a prose poem, thus aligning it more exactly with "Al Aaraaf" than might seem), and to some of the scientific and para-scientific ideas that surface in the stories and in *The Narrative of Arthur Gordon Pym*. He was keenly aware of scientific literature but feared the onslaught of what would later be called scientism.

Another of the poems accompanying "Al Aaraaf" in the second volume in an unnamed sonnet, his first in print, in which he takes to task a Science "Who alterest all things with thy peering eyes" and preys vulture-like on the poet's heart with "dull realities", a neat reworking of the Prometheus myth. The tone is rhetorical, even slightly shrill, but the closing cadences magnificently capture Poe's conviction that science is a form of unwelcome dis-enchantment.

> Hast thou not dragged Diana from her car?
> And driven the Hamadryad from the wood
> To seek a shelter in some happier star?
> Has thou not torn the Naiad from her flood,
> The Elfin from the green grass, and from me
> The summer dream beneath the tamarind tree?

This is callow enough and Poe himself consigned it with the "minor poems" of his title, but it has a vivid music commensurate with its elevation of the imagination over mere logic.

The real interest of these early poems lies not so much in their intrinsic worth as in Poe's obsessive revision of them. The oddity of "Al Aaraaf" is that it appears to have been published incomplete. He refers in correspondence to a four-part structure, but only two sections appeared in print. Quinn makes something of the abandoned sections, though a more straightforward explanation is that Poe simply rationalised the poem's diffuse architecture as he did with "Tamerlane". It appears in a new version, shortened and much improved; Poe did later reintroduce some of the deleted elements, but ultimately – and rightly – settled on the 1829 version. He did something similar with "Fairyland", a poem which seems to evoke the moss-draped landscape round Sullivan's Island in South Carolina but then moves off into a fantastical realm which anticipates the setting and the dislocated temporality of some of the great stories – "Huge moons there wax and wane / Again – again

– again-". The introduction of a human element, some forty lines added in 1831 as a prologue to the poem, entirely dispels its magic. Again, Poe later reverted to the 1829 version.

"Fairyland"'s other-worldliness was more explicitly expressed in a poem originally called "Preface" and later revised as "Romance". The former title is better, in that it reinforces the impression that Poe is making a kind of manifesto statement. Quinn suggests that in it Poe is at deliberate odds with the Wordsworthian definition of poetry in the "Preface" to the *Lyrical Ballads* (1802) as "emotion recollected in tranquillity", forgetting that in the first half of that often-quoted sentence the English poet had stated clearly "Poetry is the spontaneous overflow of powerful feelings". Though Poe acknowledges that the world intrudes too much into the imaginative realm, there is nothing to be gained from tranquil recollection. Poetry is nothing other than the sympathetic vibration of the heart.

> My heart would feel to be a crime
> Did it not tremble with the strings!

The lyre is vigorously struck in the moment of passion, not used to console and while away.

Al Araaf, Tamerlane and Minor Poems was published by Hatch & Dunning of Baltimore in December 1829. Unlike its predecessor, which had fallen unnoticed from the presses, this second collection did receive some critical attention. The mother of his friend David Hale mentioned it in *Godey's Lady's Book* and, somewhat later, published "The Visionary" there. In his search for a publisher, Poe had gone first to Professor William Wirt, a distinguished jurist and former Attorney-General of the United States, later an unsuccessful presidential candidate on the anti-Masonic ticket, who he had met at Charlottesville. Wirt gave him advice and some names who might be of use. Poe attempted to make contact with Robert Walsh, editor of the *American Quarterly Review* (a potential first contact with the world of American literary magazines which were to dominate his later career, both fruitfully and contentiously), but it seems that the young poet's approaches to Carey, Lea & Carey and to Hatch & Dunning were made without formal introduction. Nonetheless, Poe's name was becoming known. The doyen of American critics John Neal, who had made his name as an American follower of Byron, made positive noises about "E.A.P. of Baltimore", dismissing some of the shorter lyrics with a "Bah!" that must have sounded uncomfortably like the "Poh!" evoked by some of David Poe's stage performances, and expressing an understandable scepticism about Poe's self-assessment as the finest lyric voice yet to sound in the United States, but also expressing the belief that Poe's "exquisite nonsense" contained enough promise to justify the hope that the newcomer might one day make "a beautiful and perhaps magnificent poem".

On the basis of some tear-sheets from the forthcoming volume and a letter sent round by Poe explaining the origins of "Al Aaraaf", Neal also gave Poe a platform and some salutary advice in the *Yankee and Boston Literary Gazette*, suggesting that mere youthful talent and a strong aesthetic sense – Poe had made much of the fact that "I am young – not yet twenty – *am* a poet – if deep worship of all beauty can make me one …" – would not suffice if they were not matched by moral strength and unflagging application. This perhaps in direct response to Poe's initially odd confession that he had been an "idler" from childhood. The point he was trying to make was that verse had never distracted him from some worthy profession, nor that it had been taken up in defiance of parental authority, "for I have no father – nor mother".

True to the letter, but one wonders in what spirit John Allan read that freighted line. As to a profession, Poe had already abandoned one craft in favour of poetry, but despite making impressive headway, with two books published while still technically in his teens, was now about to take it up again, however temporarily.

∞∞∞

Having performed well in his first round of examinations at West Point, Poe decided on the very day of his next, mid-term tests that he had had enough of the place. On January 3 1831 – he dates the letter "1830", a common enough mistake in the early days of a new year – he wrote to his foster-father, whom he refers to as "my nominal guardian", in a familiar vein: Allan was keeping him penniless; Poe had never asked for his charity in the first place, so why offer it and then withhold it when "General" Poe would have been quite well able to offer him a comfortable home (there is no more evidence of this than there is of Allan's "promises of adoption"); wanting for necessities, let alone luxuries, he will be forced to abandon his duties and leave the academy; he will go whatever the case, but without Allan's letter of permission will be denied a final pay; and so on, self-pitying, angry, threatening, rewriting the past. Allan did not see fit to reply.

This time, though, Poe was not bluffing. At a general court-martial on January 28, he was charged with gross neglect of duty and disobedience, having failed to attend parades and musters, and having refused a direct command to attend church service. Oddly, given that his aim was to be thrown out of West Point, Poe pleaded not guilty to the first charge, but guilty to the others. In the event, all charges were proven and it was decided that Poe should be dismissed from the service. This was a decision that required ratification in Washington, but in addition the actual discharge was post-dated to the beginning of March. Poe actually left West Point some three weeks earlier than that, which would have made him technically AWOL. He was, however, suffering ill-health, with some kind of ear infection, and it may have been decided to let a troublesome cadet depart early rather than have him stagger round the parade ground or clutter up the infirmary.

No other cause of staggering other than middle-ear trouble is mentioned at this period. Whatever complaints Poe's officers had about him, drunkenness does not seem to have been among them.

∞∞∞

West Point was not Poe's last regular employment, nor was it the last time that he came into conflict with employers, but the discharge does mark an epoch in his life. For the remainder of his allotted span, and by 1820 it was already half over, he lived by his pen. In the closing lines of the standard biography, written almost a hundred years after Poe's death and still unsurpassed, Arthur Hobson Quinn delivers an astonishing but unarguable verdict: "he remains not only the one American, but also the one writer in the English language, who was at once foremost in criticism, supreme in fiction, and in poetry destined to be immortal". Poe also served as an editor, and when not taken in drink or inflamed by *ad hominem* attacks, a very effective one. And like most working writers, he was occasionally required to do hack work simply to make his way; fairly recondite hack work at that, a textbook on conchology, about which he knew nothing beyond what he may have picked up – literally – on the strand at Sullivan's Island during those long strolls where his imagination took wing.

He would certainly have had less time at West Point for writing verse than he had at Fort Moultrie, so it must be assumed that the new poems and revisions in the third collection were written in Baltimore and Richmond while he was waiting for his appointment to the academy. His preface to the volume is, however, datelined West Point and sets out in the clearest terms yet his conception of verse as something that creates an overall impression on the listener rather than delivering its insights in a linear way. The analogy he uses is that of a painting, whose brushstrokes convey nothing at close quarters but which cohere powerfully when viewed from an appropriate distance. Interestingly, while praising Coleridge, Poe rejects the metaphysical dimension of Wordsworth's poetry, suggesting that the "*immediate* object" of verse is beauty rather than truth.

The qualification is important because it confounds the casual understanding of Poe's aesthetic as an essentially amoral one, or at best one that avoids moral content. To believe that is to conflate – and very misleadingly conflate – quite separate considerations and to make an absurdly wrongheaded identification between art and life. The view follows a simple but skewed logic: Poe was immoral in life; Poe seems to argue for art that does not *in the first instance* answer to ethics; that in turn rather seems to prove Poe's immorality; and so it goes on. By contrast, accept the possibility that Poe's wickedness was more apparent than actual, and in large part an artefact of malice and misunderstanding; then put firmer emphasis on *immediate* and *in the first instance* and look again at the work to recognize that for Poe there was immorality in a bad rhyme or a fudged metre because any such lapse violates a fragile but essential unity of beauty and truth. In his fiction particularly, Poe chose to collapse any distinction between art and life, but we need to understand how that suspension of difference actually functions. Arthur Gordon Pym *is* Edgar Allan Poe, but not in the crude sense that Pym merely acts (and that word can never have an entirely neutral or innocent connotation in the context of Poe's life) as a masked proxy for the author and those of his obsession that had to be repressed for the common day. This is what excites the Freudians, D. H. Lawrence in his idiosyncratic way, Princess Marie Bonaparte in her 1933 *Edgar Poe: Etude psychanalytique,* which unwittingly did Poe's reputation as much harm as Griswold's malice. What makes Pym Poe is what makes Poe Pym, and that is the act of writing itself, an absolute moral and physical commitment to language. For Poe, the written was the real, the unwritten in consequence not.

In 1831, Pym was still some seven years in the future, but it was in 1831 that Poe, cut adrift from every tie except those of language, wounded by loss and disappointment, begins to sound a new and deeper tone in his work. Compare the exquisite nonsense of "Al Aaraaf" with a similarly inspired poem in the third collection. "Israfel" is headed by a quotation from the Koran, repeated in part in the opening stanza, declaring the title character to be the sweetest-voiced of all the angels, and one "'Whose heart strings are a lute'". Once again, Poe asserts the unWordsworthian view that poetic emotion is best expressed while the living wires are still vibrating, but there is another dimension to "Israfel" than mere passion.

Therefore thou art not wrong,
Israfeli, who despisest
An unimpassioned song;
To thee the laurels belong,
Best bard, because the wisest!
Merrily live, and long!

Wisdom is a note that has not been so clearly sounded before.

Then there is the extraordinary "The Doomed City", later revised as "The City of Sin", but best known and best titled as "The City in the Sea". In its final version, it combines virtuosic prosody with an almost conversational directness, beginning:

Lo, Death has reared himself a throne
In a strange city lying alone
Far down within the dim West,
Where the good and the bad and the worst and the best
Have gone to their eternal rest.

Here is another world turned upside down, shadowed by impenetrable cloud, lit only by phosphorescence from the "hideously serene" seas below. The place, and the cadences by which Poe evokes it, are stilled and inanimate; substance and shadow are indistinguishable. Only at the very end do the waves stir and take on a reddish glow as the cursed city settles into collapse and Hell rises to claim it. It is a foretaste of the decadent House of Usher collapsing into the dark tarn.

Apart from a passing reference to Babylon – the poem's only awkward simile and one of its few prosodic lapses – there is no attempt to identify the city or explain the curse that lies upon it. But clearly this is not Al Aaraaf or Fairyland but a human realm, indicated by "The viol, the violet, and the vine", three strong signifiers of human culture. Poe recognised early the power of indirection. Unnamed horrors are often more terrifying than those explicitly described, and here the city's fate is all the more poignant for being unexplained. It is not, by definition, one of the Cities of the Plain, utterly sunk in sin, but a place that has been home to good, bad, worst and best alike. And while there is no active human presence in the city, its attributes are subtly anthropomorphised. The poem's only repeated lines are:

Resignedly beneath the sky
The melancholy waters lie.

Resignation suggests a natural disaster, perhaps a foretaste of the plague that stalks "The Masque of the Red Death", one of Poe's best known stories. Cholera was rife in Baltimore in 1831 and probably helped inspire the story; the poem necessarily dates from rather earlier, though the line of thinking may be continuous.

From this point on in his career, he becomes the kind of phrasemaker destined to figure disproportionately in dictionaries of quotations. The much-reworked "To -- --" from 1829 yielded the lovely couplet

All that we see or seem
Is but a dream within a dream

which becomes a kind of touchstone for Poe's characteristic estrangements and alienations. In "The City in the Sea", also much reworked, Death's throne is twice associated with the melancholy resignation of the unseen population. After that repeated couplet come these lines:

> So blend the turrets and shadows there
> That all seem pendulous in air,
> While from a proud tower in the town
> Death looks gigantically down.

It is a magnificent image, chilling and archetypal; historian Barbara Tuchman borrowed *The Proud Tower* for her study of Europe's slide into the First World War. But more famous still were two lines from a poem which Poe claimed to have written in his teens in homage to Jane Stanard. In their original form, they are given as:

> To the beauty of fair Greece
> And the grandeur of old Rome

but just as Poe, a devoted student of the classics, knew that "beauty" wasn't quite the correct opposition to Rome's world-striding civilisation, he also recognised that the two adjectives blunted the couplet's impact considerably. They are now almost universally known as:

> To the glory that was Greece
> And the grandeur that was Rome

in which music and sense are perfectly balanced. "To Helen", which apostrophises Mrs Stanard as a feminine ideal, is a poem, significantly, about voyaging. Though everyone knows the following lines, almost everyone forgets that the rhyme-word for "Rome" is "home".

Poe's dreams of travel, perhaps acquired from Henry, were never to come true. Very soon, he would be part of a cramped, claustrophobic household in Baltimore, which included his grandmother, aunt, his fey brother, and the girl who would become his child-wife. In the poems of 1831, though, Poe had discovered a new voice and a new means of self-projection. "To Helen" is an unquestionably great poem, certainly in the final form that appeared in the *Saturday Museum,* a Philadelphia paper, in 1843. Quibbles about the exact meaning of "Nicean" – a reference to Nicaea or something else? – only detract from its remarkable prosody, in which control and improvisation, rule and variation are so carefully balanced. There are wonderful things elsewhere in the volume, too. "The Valley of Nis" is a variant on "The Doomed City". Later re-titled "The Valley of Unrest", it mentions the chilly seas round the Hebrides, which Poe may have glimpsed on that long ago trip to Scotland. In any of its forms, it is a vaguer, less pictorial poem than "The Doomed City"/"The City in the Sea", but its music, with a subtle variation of internal beats and alternation of couplet and triplet rhymes is unparalleled in American poetry at the time.

Poems by Edgar A. Poe: Second Edition was published by Elam Bliss of New York sometime in April 1831. The dedication is easily enough explained. Poe was not hankering after West Point and there is no mystery this time as to how he got together the money to publish his book. *Poems* was subscribed by his fellow-cadets, at the rate of 75 cents per copy printed. So, he did not lack for friends with ready pockets, and as would shortly be clear he still had blood family who would take him in. It is not clear how Poe survived in the months after his discharge from the Corps but he seems to have been brought very low indeed. The man who emerges from this period is chastened but stronger, still poor but resolute, unmistakably a man rather than a romantic boy. His verse was still in the foothills, but he had taken a great step forward both technically and expressively; his eyes were on the summits. Wisdom and ethics now weighed as heavily in his scales of value as beauty and love. Impossible to imagine the Poe of even two years previously endorsing the epigraph from Rochefoucauld which he appended to the title page of *Poems*: "*TOUT LE MONDE A RAISON*".

5

"PS I am poor": Poe and the literary life, 1831–6

One might reasonably expect the opposite to be the case, but the certifiable facts of Poe's life between 1831 and 1834 are even less clear than before. It is as if history has enforced some inverse ratio between his small but growing fame and the survival of definite evidence; or, to use a Poe image, as if some imp of the perverse has taken hold of the record, destroyed salient details and hopelessly muddled fact and fancy.

A published writer is, of course, granted some kind of foothold in the world, however insecure and precarious. Even where it is not possible to establish the details of Poe's life with any certainty, it now becomes possible at least to track his work and reactions to it. On January 14 1832, "Metzengerstein" appeared under his name in the *Philadelphia Saturday Courier*. Over the course of the year, a further four works were published in the same pages. On October 19 1833, "Manuscript Found in a Bottle" was printed in the *Baltimore Saturday Visiter*, with an enthusiastic imprimatur from an editorial board that included lawyer and future secretary of the navy

John Pendleton Kennedy, who as "Mark Littleton" had published his own first novel *Swallow Barn* the previous year.

Kennedy's enthusiasm represented one fiction writer's
admiration for another. These latest outpourings from Poe's
pen were not poems, crucially, but prose tales. "Metzengerstein" was the first of a group written during 1832 and is
in many regards the finest of them. In theme, it somewhat
resembles the later "William Wilson" in that it deals with the
reification of evil in living form, not here as a shadow self,
but as a horse that steps down from a tapestry only to bear
its terrified young hero Baron Frederick into a consuming
fire. Autobiographical elements which would soon become
resonantly obsessive themes are already present in the story
– not least the notion of hatreds passed down through a
family – but what strikes one most about "Metzengerstein",
apart from Poe's astonishingly mature avoidance of obvious
symbolism, is how technically astute the story is: perfectly
formed, atmospheric, consistently suspenseful and rising to
a genuinely shocking climax. Already the technical mastery
that would see Poe transform the modern short story was
in evidence. That he anticipated modern*ism* as well is suggested by "MS Found in a Bottle", in which naturalism and
the uncanny, the old device of a found text and the most
gripping rhetorical immediacy, classical unity of form and
an aesthetics of incompletion work together seamlessly. If it
extraordinary than a young man of 23 and 24 could write
with such maturity in a form he had only just taken up and
which had few existing English language models, it is doubly
extraordinary that he should have done so, given the conditions under which he was required to live.

∞∞∞

In Baltimore, Poe took refuge with his aunt Maria Clemm. It must have been a strange, certainly a crowded domestic scene. As well as Maria, her daughter Virginia and son Henry, the little house on Mechanics Row, Wilks Street, also sheltered Poe's grandmother, relict of the "General", and his brother William Henry, increasingly lost to drink. What they lived on, apart from Mrs David Poe's pension, is not clear. Certainly Poe could not have contributed much to the budget, though it is possible that in addition to his known publications he contributed hackwork to one of the many magazines and papers springing up in the city. He received a $50 prize from the *Visiter* in October 1833 for "MS Found in a Bottle", but "Metzengerstein" and the other stories submitted to the *Philadelphia Saturday Courier* lost out to Delia S. Bacon's more obviously popular "Love's Martyr" and when the paper's editors printed Poe's main entry in January 1832 (and then four other of his stories – "The Duke de L'Omelette", "A Tale of Jerusalem", "A Decided Loss" and "The Bargain Lost" – through the year) it is most unlikely that they paid a fee for any of them.

Money was his most pressing need, to the point of obsession, and as such, remained his last link with John Allan and his new wife. Poe certainly looked for editorial work in Baltimore. One surviving letter of application states that "Mr Allan has married again and I no longer look on Richmond as my place of residence". There are persistent rumours that Poe did return to Richmond during this period, before and after Allan's death. These can less readily dismissed than the legend of "Poe's Mary", the Mary Devereaux who allegedly had an affair with the young poet and author but managed to remain hidden to history until she popped up in a *Harper's Magazine* article published on the 40th anniversary of his death, like the present-day groupies who come out of the publishing woodwork now claiming to have had relationships with Jimi Hendrix, Jim Morrison or John Lennon or some other doomed icon no longer in a position to sue.

Poe certainly did resume badgering Allan with begging letters, written in increasing desperation. At one point, he claims to have been arrested for debt (he probably wasn't); at others, he suggests that his few funds all go to maintaining William Henry's self-destructive regiment. Throughout the renewed correspondence they oscillate between sentimentality – "when I think of the long twenty-one years that I have called you father, and you have called me son, I could cry like a child" – self-justification – "I am not idle – nor addicted to any vice" – and a veiled air of threat. "Dear Sir" does not work, so "My dear pa" takes its place. He tries to touch an emotional nerve by reminding Allan of all he times he perched the boy on his knee, then goes for a more pragmatic approach: even though he knows that all affection between them is gone and forfeit, would it not represent a reasonable investment, even if not a discharge of responsibility, to help out a struggling young man one last time?

All was to naught. Poe was now out of Richmond's sight, and out of his foster-father's mind as well. In April 1833, Poe states that it has been two years since he has received any assistance. He might have fudged emotional ties; he surely would not have stated such a thing as this if it were not the case. Poe may have made a last attempt to see Allan before his death. There is a lurid, second-hand story of him storming past Mrs Allan and breaking into the bedroom where John was dying, apparently of oedema, though apparently not too weak to threaten the younger man with a walking stick. If it happened, it came to naught. Allan's will was read at the end of March 1834. There was no mention of Edgar.

There can be no doubt that Poe was in desperate straits, but the world itself seemed turned upside down, as if in some sympathetic corollary to his distress. In 1831, Baltimore was struck by cholera, plunging the city into a state of medieval terror and perhaps providing a spark for one of his best-known stories, "The Masque of the Red Death", and for one of the more overlooked, "King Pest". Two years later the heavens offered further portents, when a spectacular meteor shower, well-documented, turned night into day, spread fear, sparked public drunkenness and near-riot, and convinced some black evangelicals that the Apocalypse was at hand. Poe may well have remembered the episode when he wrote "The Conversation of Eiros and Charmion" in 1839, a strange dialogue between daimons or angels which follows global destruction presaged by a comet, though he may also have seen Halley's Comet on its visit in 1835.

Back in 1831, the worst of the cholera struck at the end of the summer. It isn't clear whether William Henry Poe was a victim. Whatever the case, he died on August 1 and was buried at First Presbyterian Church, apparently unmissed and little mourned. Whatever bond there had been between the brothers seems to have been severed by death. One finds few recurrent references to fraternal love or conflict in the work. Poe's devotions in that household lay in a different direction.

He seems to have tutored Virginia at home, and in the course of time fallen in love with her as well, though it may well be that here his real affections were sublimated and redirected. Far from there being any evidence of dissolution at this time, Poe on the contrary must have worked fanatically hard at his writing. On April 20 1833, a week after that last despairing letter to John Allan – "For God's sake pity me and save me from destruction" – his poem "Serenade (To

Adeline)" was published in the *Visiter*. A fortnight later, he bundled up a package to the editors of the *New England Magazine*, enclosing the neatly written-out manuscript of "Epimanes" and asking that it be considered as part of a sequence of stories, "Eleven Tales of the Arabesque", a first appearance of that very Poe-ish word, but later known as "Tales of the Fiolio Club". These short narratives were supposed to be read aloud at the dinner table of an exclusive literary circle, whose members would then comment on each one in turn, "a burlesque upon criticism". A similar idea later appealed to Robert Louis Stevenson. Poe tries to exert a little leverage on the magazine's editor by stating it would not be appropriate to publish one story without the others, though he offers "Epimanes" as a free-standing text. It is an estimably controlled and professional letter, but for the hasty "PS I am poor" scrawled on the covering page.

Neither the neat submission nor the author's obvious ambition made any impact, and the *cri de coeur* went unanswered. Poe had better luck closer to home. The *Visiter*'s literary competition was announced in mid-June. Poe submitted half a dozen of his Folio Club stories, together with a poem "The Coliseum". This time, the editors gave the answer Poe was looking for, suggesting publicly that "the author owes it to his own reputation, as well as to the gratification of the community to publish the whole volume. These tales are eminently distinguished by a wild, vigorous and poetical imagination, a rich style, a fertile invention, and varied and curious learning": a first review, considered and discriminating, in fact, hard to improve upon as a summing-up of Poe's style.

Almost as important, the magazine seemed prepared to put money (or at least its readers' money) where its mouth was and back a subscribed publication of *Tales of the Folio*

Club. Poe, though, had already proposed the volume to Carey, Lee & Carey in Philadelphia, to whom he had taken "Al Aaraaf" four years earlier. He continued hawking them around for some time, though there has never been any clarity as to which stories fell under this particular rubric and the volume was never published. Poe mentions seventeen stories at one point, which may suggest that he added and subtracted to both the running order and the imaginary society's membership, which was originally given as eleven. As well as the prize-winning "The Manuscript Found in a Bottle" and "A Descent into the Maelstrom" (which is rather similar and may well have been the judges' alternative choice for the prize), the other definite inclusions must be "Epimanes", "Metzengerstein", "The Duke de L'Omelette", "Bon Bon", "A Tale of Jerusalem", "Loss of Breath", "Lionizing", "Mystification", "Shadow", "Berenice", "King Pest the First", and "Morella". Though they failed to appear in the form he intended (Carey, Lea & Cary did, however, publish "MS Found in a Bottle" a second time, in an annual and to Poe's embarrassment), he did soon find a suitable outlet for these tales.

The judges made a good choice. "The Manuscript Found in a Bottle" is a small masterpiece of suspense. The device of the found text subtly implies a fatal outcome, while the description of the ghostly Spanish ship with its phantom crew who seem indisposed to see narrator, almost as if *he* and not they were the shade, is developed in what was to become Poe's characteristic blend of naturalism and supernaturalism. The story's opening lines are revealing. "Of my country and of my family I have little to say. Ill-usage and length of years have driven me from the one, and estranged me from the other." The narrator does, however, quickly establish that "hereditary wealth" has afforded him an excellent education, a delight in the "German moralists" and a reputation for Pyrrhonism, the kind of radically empirical world-view one might want for a character about to be exposed to strange events. Already, Poe is aware that self-revelation has to bow to the needs of narrative, a crisp warning not to read too much of the life from the fiction.

The dramatic, perfectly weighted climax of the prize-winning story, written as if at the moment of death in the great whirlpool – "amid a roaring, and bellowing and thundering of ocean and of tempest, the ship is quivering – Oh God! and – going down!" – is echoed in "The Descent Into The Maelstrom". This is a later story, though there have been some attempts to suggest it belongs to this early group of tales, presumably because of a similarity of theme, though the second tale, published in 1841, is set off the Norwegian coast rather off Java. Both show Poe's interest in and skill in evoking states which hover between the rational and irrational, and states of mind which partake of what Freud called *das Unheimliche*, inadequately translated as "the uncanny".

Something of the same happens in "Berenice", where the narrator retreats from reality by means of self-hypnosis, and views the world around him with an infantile fixation that would be familiar to students of post-Freudians like Melanie Klein and Jacques Lacan a century later. This narrative stance, dreamy, morally latent, and indiscriminately obsessive, is more important to an understanding of Poe's writing than the tale's more notorious and more readily analysable theme. The narrator is engaged to his cousin who he does not love and regards as morally inferior. Most casual commentators view the story as an early realisation of Poe's belief that the death of a woman (physically, if not spiritually, beautiful in this case) is the most poetic subject, and follow that cue through a narrative that involves premature burial and (in one version) the violent removal of Berenice's teeth from her still-breathing body. In psychoanalytic terms, this is almost too orthodox and mars the tale's potential subtlety. What Poe is striving to understand here is the nature of identity and the existence of a soul or spiritual nature beyond the physical frame which may simply contain it or – and this is one of the deepest questions Poe poses – may help define it.

The story is ultimately unsuccessful, and Poe later dismissed it as a fancy written on a wager that he could not produce a serious tale on a subject so horrific. His troubled and troubling examination of what later would be described as the psychosomatic unity of human existence was better handled in "Morella", which all critics recognise as an early draft of what was to be his greatest story, "Ligeia". In this early version, subsequently revised for a proposed collection of *Phantasy Pieces*, Morella is the narrator's philosophical equal and shares his urge to understand what survives of the self after death. They have a child, who seems uncannily – that inadequate word again – similar to the mother, who dies. Poe originally left the story at this point, poised again between the naturalistic understanding that childbirth is still a dangerous business and a more metaphysical speculation about the moral co-existence of two such similar souls. Later versions press the point more fully, with the revelation of Morella's empty tomb and her ghostly (or physical) response to the calling of her name at her daughter's baptism, but the earlier version has a hauntingly ambiguous quality which is superior.

Similar themes are attempted in the parable "Shadow", a superb example of Poe's skills as a prose poet but also of his evolving awareness that writing itself is a form not so much of self-revelation as of self-extinction. It begins "Ye who read are still among the living; but I who write shall have long since gone my way into the region of shadows." This might be understood as a forlorn struggler's recognition that only posterity would acknowledge his virtues, but there is a deeper meaning to it than that. The text's biblical cadences, underlined by an epigraph from the Psalms and the deathly speech beginning "'I am SHADOW ...'", are obvious enough, as is the foreshadowing of later, more developed accounts of the plague but what is consistently fascinating about the piece, which occupies no more than two or three pages of type, is Poe's consistent concern with intermediate states of being and a romantic mirroring of earthbound concerns in the cosmic realm.

Nothing else in that early sequence is of the same quality as these. "King Pest" is lightweight and derivative (of Disraeli's *Vivian Grey*, published anonymously in 1826, much pirated in America and probably of interest to Poe because of its background in the founding of a newspaper). "Lionizing" touches on the same world, a satire on literary puffs and flyting, but palpably the work of a young man who wants to join the world he is satirising. "Mystification" (or "Von Jung") is a swipe at the vogue for duelling, again spoken in the voice of an ambitious outsider. And "Epimanes", so carefully written out in that first submission to the *New England Magazine*, is a slender fable, a curious blend of "The Emperor's New Clothes" and classical mythology. It isn't clear why Poe should have considered it the best candidate for publication in 1833.

∞∞∞∞

The blurted postscript to the editors of the *New England Magazine* underlines the salient fact of Poe's life at this time. Money was an abiding obsession and drove Poe's frenzy of literary activity as much as creative inspiration did. The $50 prize from the *Visiter* must have been uncommonly welcome, though typically Poe felt aggrieved that he did not win a further $25 for his poem "The Coliseum" (with some justice, given that the verse prize went to the magazine's editor John H. Hewitt who submitted "The Song of the Winds" under the name "Henry Wilton", a questionable action though perfectly allowable given that Hewitt was not one of the judges and that pseudonymous submissions were explicitly allowed). If "The Coliseum" really were placed second – and it was published in the next edition of the *Visiter* – then Poe could claim some kind of moral victory, though the incident may have served more to fuel his growing paranoia about magazine politics.

Almost as important as the prize and the small literary cachet that came with it was the introduction to John Pendleton Kennedy, who at less than forty was perhaps too youthful to assume the role of father-figure, but who certainly became a stout supporter of Poe's talent. After the announcement of the prize, the young author apparently went to Kennedy's house to thank him personally, striking the older man as a mixture of self-confidence and grave melancholy. Kennedy said later that he had opened his home and table to Poe, whom he found to be in a state of near-starvation. Poe was also allowed to use Kennedy's own horse for exercise. He lent him money in addition, though Poe exerted characteristic leverage in this regard, seeming to decline a dinner invitation because of his personal appearance – others who remember him at the period say his dress was shabby but meticulous

– but adding that, were a loan of $20 to be forthcoming, he might be able to accept after all.

Most significant of all Kennedy's kindnesses was an introduction to Thomas Wylkes (or Willis) White, the proprietor of the *Southern Literary Messenger*, who could only have been intrigued by Kennedy's description of Poe as "highly imaginative and a little *terrific*". He went on to say that Poe was writing a tragedy – this was the ill-fated *Politian*, written less with his actor parents in mind than with a belief characteristic among American writers from Poe to Henry James (and arguably beyond when the movies came into being) that the only real literary success was success on the stage – but that for the moment he was "drudging" at hack-work. Kennedy passed on some small sums of money from White, probably for book reviews.

A printer by profession, White had launched the *Messenger* in the summer of 1834, bent on raising the literary tastes of Southerners. Understandably, given that high-minded mission, White may have originally disliked the masochistic tone of "Berenice" – which begins "Misery is manifold. The wretchedness of earth is multiform" – but he published it in March 1835, beginning a vitally important association. Poe set about making himself indispensable, placing puff notices about the *Messenger* in other publications, writing reviews and advising White on matters of magazine publication with an astonishing confidence. He points out – and, as Quinn comments, this tends to confound any notion of Poe as a solitary genius, standing apart from the literary values of his time – that the public seemed to want precisely the kind of story "Berenice" was, "the ludicrous heightened into the grotesque: the fearful coloured into the horrible: the witty exaggerated into the burlesque: the singular wrought out into the strange and mystical". He mentions in passing that Kennedy is of a similar mind and proposes to send White a similar tale each month.

Whether genuinely impressed or simply browbeaten, White accepted. "Morella" appeared in the *Messenger* in April 1834, one month after "Berenice", with the literary skit "Lionizing" and "Hans Phaal, a Tale" in the two subsequent issues. The last of these is presumably the story (later retitled "The Adventure of One Hans Pfaall") Kennedy remember Poe enthusing over on one of their first meetings. Asked "What are you writing now?", Poe replied "'*A Voyage To the Moon*'" and began to describe the tale and its scientific apparatus with some excitement, speaking in the first person as he fantasised about leaving the earth and travelling ever higher until the balance of gravity changed and he was drawn upwards by the moon's own force. It is a significant tale in two important respects, drawing strongly on Poe's desire for sublimation and transcendence, but also his willingness to locate it in the known laws of natural science.

ooooo

In mid-1835 White wrote and asked Poe to work as assistant editor on the *Messenger*. By the end of a summer that saw the death of his grandmother (another symbolic desertion by the female) he was back in Richmond again, doubtless with mixed feelings. There were sour memories, but there were also old friends, including the now-married Elmira Shelton.

Poe's duties at the magazine were initially unspecific and *ad hoc*, and White was at pains to make it clear that he was not being offered the editorship. He had some reason to be cautious, as will be seen below, and the initial arrangement was for one month only. At Christmas 1835, White wrote in the magazine that the "intellectual" – in other words, editorial – "department of the paper is under the conductor of the proprietor assisted by a gentleman of distinguished literary talents". He then mentions Poe by name, as if the writer of tales whose work appeared in the *Messenger* both anonymously (for new work) and signed (for previously published pieces) were different to the distinguished gentleman "seconding" the proprietor. There had been two previous editors, the playwright James E. Heath and, much more briefly, Edward V. Sparhawk, who may have overlapped with Poe in the summer of 1835. Though Heath had worked without a salary or honorarium, it seems that White paid Poe a salary of $520 per annum, which later rose to something closer to $60 per month.

Poe was now tasting the literary life proper, able to correspond with fellow authors as an equal and to wield a certain power over them. He also began to theorise a little about the nature of story-telling, particularly in grotesque forms, and about prosody, though here his lack of a classical education and autodidactic approach to versification are immediately obvious. This was also a reciprocal process Perhaps recognising that Poe was flexing his muscles as a critic, Kennedy tells him in February 1836: "You are strong enough now to be criticised. Your fault is your love of the extravagant. Pray beware of it." Kennedy had become a confidant, expressing sympathy for Poe's "blue devils" and private woes, of which more in the next chapter, but also one of the few from whom the very assured young writer might have taken such a comment, however ingratiating his written replies to other commentators sometimes are.

Unfortunately, perhaps, Poe not only flexed his critical

muscles, but also raised ungloved fists. He was not the first literary critic in America, but he was certainly one of the very first from a non-establishment class. That freed him from a certain consensus tone, which was very formal, very proper, often more concerned with social morality than with aesthetics, and strenuously resistant to both critical grandstanding (almost all reviews at the time, and for a long time after were unsigned) and *ad hominem* attacks. Poe set about abandoning these conventions, and it was good for business.

Though White seemed determined to keep Poe in his place, he was quickly aware that critical maulings are great talking points in a literate society and always far more entertaining to write and read. In December 1835 Poe wrote a swingeing account of *Norman Leslie*, a now unreadable melodrama by Theodore S. Fay. The review caused more of a stir than the book, not least because Fay was an editor at a rival paper, the *New York Mirror*. Conscious perhaps that the South had a new literary bulldog, White quietly slipped his young assistant's leash. By the turn of the year, Poe was editor in all but name. By the time he left White's employ a year later, the circulation of the *Southern Literary Messenger* had gone up from around five hundred copies to more than three thousand. Newspaper and magazine circulation is an occult science and it is hard to determine whether the high figure is testament to Poe's natural genius or whether the low figure is just another warning that proprietors should stick to business and leave editorial issues to those gifted in that area. Certainly, Poe's letters to White suggest that he knew instinctively what would and what would not best serve the paper. His later success at *Graham's* in Philadelphia suggests this first success was no fluke.

White listened to him for a time and together they

prospered, though the magazine always seems to have been commercially marginal. White severed the relationship in January 1837; he spoke of Poe having "retired" from the post, but this may be polite *pro forma*. There is strong evidence that Poe was drinking heavily. A stern but affectionate letter of September 1835 from White (it was written while Poe was back in Baltimore and is signed as from "your true Friend") expresses some concern that if he returns to Richmond "you would again sip the juice, even till it stole away your senses". It isn't a throwaway reference. A few lines later, he speaks more warmly: "You have fine talents Edgar, and you ought to have them respected, as well as yourself. Learn to respect yourself, and you will very soon find that you are respected. Separate yourself from the bottle, and bottle companions, for ever!" It is clear that Poe has been put on some kind of probation, which he later violated. White makes it clear that even if Poe does return to Richmond, he has received his last warning: "it must be especially understood by us that all engagements on my part would be dissolved the moment you get drunk". The personal part of the letter ends alarmingly: "No man is safe who drinks before breakfast! No man can do so, and attend to business properly". Can it be that Poe was turning up at the office already intoxicated? Given the heat and persistence of his tone, White cannot simply have been reacting to rumour or warnings about Poe's past history. Poe himself referred at the time to a recent "illness" which is not otherwise specified but which clearly kept him from his duties. In a letter written in 1841 (unfortunately on April 1) Poe reacts robustly to rumours about his drinking, apparently being put round in Philadelphia by a subsequent editor and employer. Interestingly here, Poe admits that he did have an episode of drunkenness in Richmond, which he blames on

"Southern conviviality", but insists that he is now sober: "My sole drink is water".

There may have been other factors in Poe's departure. With the hindsight of a few years, he remembered that "the drudgery was excessive, the salary was contemptible", though given how desperate his straits had been, he must have been grateful for both work and money at the time. More important perhaps, Poe's personal circumstances were dramatically changed, and while White seems to have amenable to some increase in his assistant's honorarium, he did also voice some concerns about who exactly controlled the magazine, proprietor or assistant editor. Then again, it may simply be that having overcome his immediate crisis, Poe simply felt constrained or, like many a desk-bound literary man, merely wished to spend more time writing his own work and less reviewing that of others. One biographer estimates that in his year at the *Messenger* Poe wrote just three stories and six poems, but eighty-three reviews. He was also contributing articles on every subject under the Southern sun, including the education system (which he deplored), slavery (which he supported), ancient history, politics, intellectual puzzles, philology and chess.

Perhaps the most important notice he contributed to the paper was written right at the beginning of his association, when he contributed a notice to the February 1835 edition, reviewing Robert Montgomery Bird's historical novel *Calavar*. On that occasion, Poe took as his text Sydney Smith's famous rhetorical put-down "Who reads an American book?" In what followed, and insistently in his book notices for the *Messenger* Poe reminded his countrymen that, fifty years after Yorktown, secession from the colonial power was still incomplete. "In letters as in Government we require a declaration of independence", adding with the aggressive tone that would become typical of his polemical writing, "A better thing still would be a declaration of war". Typically, Poe made no move to unite his fellow-American writers behind him. Instead of launching barbs at the continuing British hegemony over polite literature, he launched into his compatriots. "There is not a more disgusting spectacle under the sun than our sub-serviency to British criticism. It is disgusting, first because it is truckling, servile, pusillanimous, secondly because of its gross irrationality." Poe ruthlessly pointed up the fundamen-tal inconsistencies and hypocrisies of the situation, reminding his readers that the only American writers to receive support in the British prints – and Poe studied *Blackwood's* and other journals carefully – were those who "have either openly paid homage to English institutions, or have had lurking at the bottom of their hearts a secret principle at war with Democ-racy:- we know all this, and yet, day after day, submit our necks to the degrading yoke of the crudest opinion that ema-nates from the fatherland" – a telling choice of term! – "We complain of our want of an International Copyright on the ground that this want justifies our publishers in inundating us with British opinion in British books: and yet when these very publishers at their own obvious risk, and even obvious loss, do publish an American book, we turn up our noses at it with supreme contempt, until it has been dubbed 'read-able' by some illiterate Cockney critic." This is strong stuff, as significant in its way and quite on a par for pure venom with Lord Byron's "English Bards and Scotch Reviewers", which Poe would certainly have known.

Some contemporaries were, of course, striving to create a strong indigenous American literature on their own terms. Kennedy had made a modest start with *Swallow Barn* and

Horse-Shoe Robinson; Poe gave the latter a lacklustre review in the *Messenger*. More significantly, shut away in the "owl's nest" of his family home, Nathaniel Hawthorne was writing what would become the *Twice-Told Tales*, published first individually in magazines and then in book form under that name, in 1837. Poe later took Hawthorne to task for his dependence on allegory, but one senses that he was also squaring up to a rival. His literary antennae were too fine to overlook the quality of those haunting tales. His instinct for conflict was also too well developed not to recognise that Hawthorne and Henry Wadsworth Longfellow, a profound hate figure for Poe, were in alliance, Northern mandarins who automatically despised anything that crawled out of the South.

These men, both younger than himself, had something else that Poe coveted, a measure of financial security and sense of belonging to the social fabric. Longfellow was made the first professor of modern languages at Bowdoin College, a post that allowed him to travel to Europe (and later write *Outre-Mer* in consequence); it was there he met the slightly older Hawthorne. In 1835 was given the chair of French and Spanish at Harvard. Though Hawthorne was content to dream his life away at home, he too required regular employment and in 1839 was taken on as weigher and gauger at the Boston Custom House. It wasn't inspiring work, but it kept the wolf from the door. Even before that, and at exactly the time Poe was hawking round his *Tales from the Folio Club* a friend of Hawthorne's had offered to put up $250 to underwrite any possible loss from the *Twice-Told Tales*.

Poe had neither patron nor parental support, and only insecurely paid employment. Though he continued to pursue non-literary jobs now and in the years ahead, he was fated to live by his pen, turning his hand to whatever would command a fee. It is a precarious existence even for a single man, but that was no longer Poe's estate.

6

"My darling little wifey": Poe and Virginia, 1836–9

The newspaper notice is straightforward enough to attract no particular attention. "Married, on Monday, May 16th [1836], by the Reverend Mr. Converse, Mr. Edgar A. Poe to Miss Virginia Eliza Clemm." Other than the strange circumstances of his death a dozen years later, nothing in Poe's life has been more obsessively discussed, vilified, and fantasized over than his marriage to "my own sweetest Sissy, my darling little wifey". These words were actually written some months before the actual ceremony, adding weight to a rumour that Edgar and Virginia were secretly married in Baltimore in September 1835 by a future Episcopal bishop. It appears that a license was issued – or sought – at the time, but not acted upon.

The actual marriage bond of $150 (which may have been paid with money borrowed from Poe's uncle George Jr, who thought he was contributing to a rooming house Mrs Clemm proposed to open) was filed in Richmond on the day of the wedding by Poe and his friend Thomas W. Cleland, who made oath that Virginia was "of the full age of twenty-one years". She was, in fact, some three months short of her 14th birthday, which made Cleland either a dupe or a perjurer. What it made Poe himself is harder to fathom. There are various scenarios in play here. It has been suggested that Mrs Clemm suggested and promoted the match to keep the family together and to keep Edgar close to her. Alternatively, it may be that Edgar married Virginia because, by some displacement of emotion, he was in love with "Dear Aunty". However, it seems clear from the available evidence, carefully marshalled by Arthur Hobson Quinn, that Poe genuinely loved his cousin and with a passion that rises above the adolescent, even if the tone of some letters does not.

The actual spark for his decision to marry Virginia was the news that a kinsman, Neilson Poe, who was almost exactly the same age as Edgar and already married to a Clemm half-sister, had offered to take Virginia in and sponsor her education. It seems as though Neilson had also had word of a growing affection between Virginia and the worrisome Edgar (Mrs Clemm may well have been playing a double-game in all this) and was anxious to head it off. Poe's response to the news is anguished, almost hysterical. He writes blinded with tears, says his life is at an end and strikes the familiar note of living "Among strangers with *not one soul to love me*". Then almost immediately he snaps into practicality, talking of a house he has procured, "newly done up and with a large garden", and offers a detailed breakdown of his increased income and carefully managed outgoings, exactly like a proper suitor establishing his eligibility. He even re-opens the letter to enclose $5. He concludes in the same emotional tone: with Neilson, Virginia may well enjoy "accomplishments" and enter society, but no one could love her as Edgar does; and he throws himself on Virginia's mercy in his sign-off and in a postscript to his beloved: "My love, my own sweetest

Sissy, my darling little wifey, think well before you break the heart of your cousin Eddy".

It worked. Eddy and Sissy were married at a Mrs Yarrington's house by the Rev. Amasa Converse (who apparently turned a blind eye to the bride's youth) and the couple spent a short honeymoon in Petersburg, Virginia. The irregularities of the ceremony were corrected somewhat later by legal means. The moral ambiguity has proved harder to rub out. Very early marriage is not unknown, either anthropologically or historically. Marriage within the family group, likewise. Both may seem abhorrent by modern standards, tinged by a contemporary fixation on paedophilia, and by a considerable weight of misinformation regarding the risks attendant on inbreeding. However, and without any casual recourse to historical relativism, Poe's society was not like our own. In early 19th century America, populations were still small and relatively static (Poe moved around more than most of his contemporaries); family groups were more cohesive than now; mortality was high. Racial considerations and a deep undercurrent of anxiety about sexual "contagion" – which could mean anything from coloured blood to syphilis – tended to encourage early marriage. Had Poe not been a writer of the grotesque, his choice of bride would surely not have attracted such prurient attention. His marriage to Virginia seems disproportionately significant because it fits so readily into an evolving personal legend: drinker, dabbler in black arts, and now a seducer of young girls as well. Life and work strike up a familiar dissonant harmony.

Very little is known about the progress of Poe's affection for Virginia, or its sexual component, though something can be deduced even from the obscurities of "Ulalume", published after her death. There were no children, but nothing can be deduced from that. All that can be said with any certainty is that there was a strong and deep bond between the couple, who seem to have been devoted to each other. Virginia's long dying, after the haemorrhage of 1842, was an agony to Poe and certainly hastened his own decline. Those who observed them at this time, including the Scottish-born bookseller William Gowans, who lodged with the Poes and Mrs Clemm in New York during 1837, report a good man and husband and a wife of "matchless beauty and loveliness". Perhaps Gowans, too, was smitten with Virginia because he then warms to his theme: "her eye could match that of any houri, and her face defy the genius of a Canova to imitate ... she seemed as much devoted to [Poe] and his every interest as a young mother is to her first born".

In giving himself away, Gowans may have stumbled across something else. If Virginia was a child-bride, her husband was the eternal adolescent, hungry for attention and comfort. One of those he had turned to for support in the past, John Pendleton Kennedy, had noted Poe acting as his cousin's tutor and he may have redoubled his efforts after warding off the challenge of Neilson Poe. Whether Virginia afforded him much in the way of intellectual company is to be doubted, which may be why Poe turned in later years to the company of older and artistically accomplished women, though mostly – while Virginia lived – in an idealised and platonic way similar to his boyish infatuation with Mrs Jane Craig Stanard. Others who observed them at the time, including the Scottish born bookseller William Gowans, who lodged with the Poes and Mrs Clemm in New York, report a devoted couple and a relationship apparently unmarred by alcohol.

Poe had taken the family north in the early weeks of 1837. Mrs Clemm took in boarders. Poe presumably wrote and hawked round his talents. New York was more than ten times the size of Richmond but though it would have seemed to offer far more in the way of publishing, reviewing and editorial opportunities, Poe's time there is strangely quiet. He did some writing for the *New York Review*, but failed to secure a regular berth. Only a couple of short stories were published in the same period, "Von Jung, the Mystic" in the June edition of the *American Monthly Magazine*, and "Siope – A Fable", which appeared in an annual published that autumn back in Baltimore. Slim pickings for his hard work.

There are a number of possible explanations, ranging from the personal to the broadly economic. At the simplest level, the 28 year old Southerner came to New York with a certain reputation for ruffling feathers. It is quite possible that doors were closed to him as payback for harsh notices in the Virginia press. Those who live by the critical sword often find it pointing back towards them, and Poe's successful stewardship of the *Messenger* had been at the cost of making enemies elsewhere. However, the Poes and Mrs Clemm also arrived in New York on the cusp of a financial panic that would plunge the country into a recession that would last, with only a brief recovery in 1838 and 1839, for six years. Of more than 800 banks in the United States, almost 350 were forced out of business, and an estimated $100,000,000 was wiped out in New York alone. This was not a comfortable time for a jobbing writer. In a beleaguered economy, magazines and particularly books are a low domestic priority.

It is also possible that Poe was relatively quiet during 1837 because he was embarked on a larger than usual project. Having started out as a lyric poet, diversified as a writer of grotesque and arabesque tales and as a literary critic and essayist, he was now writing a novel. This in itself cannot account for much of his writing time in 1837 because presumably much of the book was written back in Richmond. Some accounts suggest that Poe was challenged to write a longer text by a publisher, Harper & Brothers in New York, who had rejected some of his stories. Whatever the case, two instalments of the novel were published in the *Messenger,* the last of them just as the family left the South. It is possible that Poe spent much of the year re-writing and re-shaping a longer text than any he had previously attempted. It appears that Harpers tried to dissuade Poe from publishing the whole novel as a serial in the *Messenger* since that would inevitably affect sales, though that in itself does not imply the book was finished or even half-written before the first instalment appeared in January. All that can be said with certainty is that the novel was contracted in June but only published (perhaps delayed by the financial crisis) thirteen months later.

The short and familiar form of the book's title is *The Narrative of Arthur Gordon Pym, of Nantucket*. To that, either Poe or his publishers attached a 106-word subtitle or "argument" that is worth quoting in full: "comprising the details of a mutiny and atrocious butchery on board the American brig *Grampus*, on her way to the South Seas, in the month of June 1827. With an account of the recapture of the vessel by the survivers; their shipwreck and subsequent horrible sufferings from famine; their deliverance by means of the British schooner *Jane Guy*; the brief cruise of his latter vessel in the Antarctic Ocean; her capture, and the massacre of her crew among a group of islands in the eighty-fourth parallel of Southern latitude; together with the incredible adventures and discoveries still farther south to which that distressing calamity gave rise."

It was evidently hoped, in line with Poe's confidence in

the selling power of horror, that this catalogue of suffering would attract readers. Unfortunately, the scientific particularity of some of the book's elements set against its supernatural climax led some early critics to condemn it as far-fetched or, swallowing the conceit of a non-fiction narrative, a hoax. No author's name appeared on the title page and Poe wrote a last-minute preface explaining that the *Messenger* extracts had only appeared under his name and in the guise of fiction from the fear that the reading public would doubt the credibility of the contents and their status as a real autobiographical narrative. This is wonderfully circular, almost "post-modern", though it seems that Poe's and Harper & Brothers' main motivation was commercial rather than ironic playfulness. He did, however, learn something from the exercise – apart from the economic unviability of novel-writing in 1837 – and it came out in a later story, now known as "The Balloon Hoax", which again played with "fact" and fiction.

There is actually rather more to *Arthur Gordon Pym* than that unflinching argument suggests. Though it has obvious affinities to both "MS Found In A Bottle" and "Descent Into The Maelstrom", its premises and development are significantly different. It begins with the young Pym – whose name has, of course, almost exactly the same cadence as Edgar Allan Poe – putting out drunk in a dinghy with his friend Augustus Barnard. They are capsized in a storm and rescued by a whaleboat returning to Nantucket. A new kind of intoxication follows, as Arthur learns that Augustus will be joining his father on the *Grampus* to make an exploratory voyage to the southern ocean. This draws quite explicitly on a real Congressional report made by Jeremiah Reynolds in 1836 proposing just such a voyage, and chapter sixteen even extensively quotes this. His decision to stow away is almost foiled by his grandfather, though Pym manages to convince the old man that he has mistaken a stranger for his grandson; another of the book's small but subtle alienating devices. On board, Pym suffers a strange torpor, apparently caused by the poisonous atmosphere below decks, but also reflective of the moral evil that has overtaken the ship. Augustus has brought Pym's dog Tiger on board and the creature finds and revives his dying master. Later, Tiger also brings Pym a letter from Augustus, written in blood, warning him to remain hidden at all costs.

It transpires that mutineers have taken over the ship and killed some of the crew. One of them, Dirk Peters, has spared Augustus. The three hatch a plan whereby Pym, who is not known to the mutineers, puts on the clothes of one of the dead sailors and pretends to be his ghost. The three retake control of the ship, killing all but one of the mutineers. From here, the book moves into what D. H. Lawrence, in another context and of another early American writer, calls a "decrescendo of reality", though without the counterbalancing "crescendo of beauty" he found in James Fenimore Cooper's work. The connection isn't an arbitrary one, since Poe's handling of cannibal savages in the later chapters of the novel is worth comparing with Cooper's treatment of the Mohicans and their adversaries. It is also worth comparing it with Herman Melville's tales of South Sea wanderings, *Typee* and *Omoo*, which were published towards the end of Poe's life in 1846 and 1847.

Melville's narratives were based on his own real-life experiences. Poe, on the other hand, had to rely somewhat on Reynolds, somewhat on Benjamin Morrell's *Narrative of Four Voyages to the South Seas and the Pacific*, which had been published in 1832, and largely on his own imagination. There is, however, something strongly in common between Poe's technique here and that of Melville later in *Moby-Dick* where the almost obsessive accretion of detail in the notorious "cetology" chapters suddenly flip-flops quantitative into qualitative, mundane detail into transcendence, when the symbolic White Whale is eventually encountered. Poe follows a similar course, piling on detail in an effort to establish the veracity of his story, but also softening up the reader for Pym's strange epiphany at the very end of the book, where Poe draws on the (at the time still credible) theory of a Hollow Earth with openings at both poles leading to a habitable inner surface to confront his narrator with a figure whose symbolic significance and ambiguities still exercise critics as much as Melville's.

The final pages of the novel are taken as from Pym's journals. With Peters and a savage called Nu-Nu who has escaped with them from the cannibal island, he begins to drift "with a hideous velocity" further into the southern ocean and towards an ambiguous "cataract" or chasm, which seems to open into yawning but momentary rents "within which was a chaos of flitting and indistinct images". Giant white birds fly out from beyond the veil, and their screaming cries make Nu-Nu die of fright. "And now we rushed into the embraces of the cataract, where a chasm threw itself open to receive us. But there arose in our pathway a shrouded human figure, very far larger in its proportions than any dweller among men. And the hue of the skin of the figure was of the perfect whiteness of the snow."

There the novel ends, and as Quinn rightly points out, it ends with an image that persists in the mind long after other details of the book have faded. Interestingly, though, many commentators on the book have assumed that the figure is female, when there is no such indication to that effect. One notes that Pym/Poe doesn't merely describe the figure as "huge" or "vast", but even *in extremis* has the presence of mind to register its disproportionate size relative to the two humans it is about to welcome, or to destroy. All is shimmering uncertainty here – are the birds real birds or phantoms? is the ashy shower volcanic dust, or powdery snow? (in the 1960s more than one noted a likeness to description of nuclear fall-out) what are the images that flicker in and out? – but, unlike those early stories which draw on a broadly similar situation, it is rendered with something approaching calm. The only exclamation mark in the final paragraph entry is attached to the birds' cry "*Tekeli-li!*" and Pym betrays no fear or other strong emotion.

It seems clear from Poe's other writings that the shrouded figure represents not so much mere physical death as the same kind of ontological extinction and absolute moral emptiness as Melville's White Whale. The confusion of Poe/Pym is in part an editorial sleight-of-hand (Poe claimed to have had letters from *Messenger* readers insisting that some elements of what was at first presented as fiction were actually true), but it also perversely points up some autobiographical dimensions of the story. Some are obvious, even glaringly so. In the opening chapter, the boys first set sail from Edgartown, on Martha's Vineyard, which almost serves as a hidden signature within the narrative. Perhaps more significantly, though, Poe makes it clear that the events described begin in June 1827. This was when he himself struck out alone as a young army cadet, either rejected by or escaping from his foster family; with this in mind, the tiny episode of Arthur's brush with his grandfather takes on a new meaning. Author and protagonist merge and separate in the most intriguing way, but with nothingness rather than self-discovery at the end of the journey.

When *Arthur Gordon Pym* was published in the United

Kingdom, by George Palmer Putnam, that extraordinary final paragraph was omitted as being too far fetched; the editors added a note explaining that the text was cut short because of Pym's demise. This only served to confirm the pattern of criticism back home in America. If Poe and Harper & Brothers hoped to make money with *Arthur Gordon Pym,* they were to be sorely disappointed. In Philadelphia *Burton's Gentlemen's Magazine* dismissed the story as pointlessly gruesome and riddled with error. He seemed to regret that Poe should be in any way involved with such a transparent effort to fool the public. William Burton, if it was he who wrote the review, was quick to forgive, however, for within two years Poe was working on *Burton's* (which changed its name to *Graham's*) again as an assistant editor, and it was there he published some of his greatest stories, including "The Fall of the House of Usher" and the no less autobiographical "William Wilson".

Less forgiving was Lewis Gaylord Clark in a review in *The Knickerbocker.* As Sidney P. Moss recounts in his valuable 1963 account of *Poe's Literary Battles,* Clark was one of the rivals with whom Poe later feuded. He found some good things in *Arthur Gordon Pym* but attacked Poe's style, and most fatally, his "slip-shod" construction. This has become a virtual consensus, which compares the allegedly slack sense of form and inconsistent mood of Poe's only finished novel with the lapidary finish and virtuosically sustained uniformity of tone in the tales. It is, however, an unfair criticism. There is every sign that Poe worked very hard at *Pym* and devoted considerable energy toward giving the book a very detailed structure in which the mood of each chapter is exactly mirrored in the corresponding chapter at the end of the book. It is hardly surprising in the context of the time that such a device – if it was a conscious stratagem at all – was not noticed by busy hacks and editors. Poe had to wait until well into the 20th century, and for the work of critics like Daniel Hofmann, whose 1972 *PoePoePoePoePoePoePoe* is a revisionist classic, for such qualities to be clearly identified and understood.

Though his English readers were led to dismiss him as a prankster, Poe had more sensitive readers on continental Europe. Chief among them was the French poet Charles Baudelaire, who was drawn by Poe's embrace of irrationality and his forensic detailing of the strange and uncanny as if he were reporting straightforward events. Unfortunately, Baudelaire – and Stephane Mallarme – also did much to establish the cult of Poe as a *poete maudit*, a pre-existentialist vivisector with a deep interest in morbid psychology, intoxication and self-destruction. Baudelaire nonetheless made a remarkable translation of Poe's novel and in homage to the American rendered the opening line as "*Mon nom est Arthur Gordon Pym*" rather than the idiomatic "*Je m'appelle …*" Critics ever since have debated the exact significance of those words, as of Melville's extraordinary opening to *Moby-Dick*: "Call me Ishmael".

ooooo

Either before or shortly after the publication of his novel, Poe moved the family to Philadelphia. The exact reasons are not clear. While the city that had seen the founding of the United States was hardly a political or cultural backwater, it had ceded much of its authority to Washington, DC, and to the rapidly growing Northern cities, and its geographical position placed it in a buffer position between their modernising instincts and the agrarian politics and vested interests of the Southern states who held the balance of power in antebellum

America. Despite unrest that sometimes spilled over into violence, Philadelphia was a quieter berth than New York and it provided the background to Poe's most productive, peaceful and optimistic years, during which he wrote some of his greatest stories, planned to set himself up as a publisher and even put out prospectuses for a new literary magazine of his own before he threw in his lot (or threw away a fortune by his way of it) with Burton.

Some, obeying D. H. Lawrence's famous injunction to trust the tale rather than the teller, have suggested that the blackness, sadism and sheer perversity of Poe's stories reveal the man inside, but it seems that in Philadelphia his life attained a measure of equilibrium, even peace, with Virginia. They moved house several times, though the precise social geography, which can only partly be reconstructed, is not particularly enlightening as to the Poes' economic or social standing at the time. They seem to have been content and secure enough. The few glimpses one has of their domestic life suggests nothing sinister, though these, of course, are mostly supplied by Poe himself in letters to professional contacts, hardly the place for personal confidences. The familiar riposte to any suggestion that Poe was a drunk and a laudanum user has always been that no writer of such productivity, as well as gifts, could possibly have spent much time helplessly inebriated. It is a fine, commonsensical argument, but it hardly helps establish an exact chronology for the work.

For periods in Philadelphia, Poe wrote less – even if he wrote sublimely well – than at other times in his life. One can often only reliably determine output by reference to actual publication, but when he had no editorial leverage or columns of his own to fill Poe often had to hawk round stories before they were eventually accepted, and this led to delays between presumed completion and publication. "Ligeia" appeared in print shortly after the family moved to Philadelphia, too shortly, one supposes, to have been written there. It was, in any case, taken by a Baltimore journal, the *American Museum,* which paid $10 for one of his greatest stories. Since it was modelled closely on "Morella", which had been published three years previously, it is possible that Poe had worked on it steadily since then, or perhaps had seen a way of breaking through some of the unresolved narrative problems of the earlier story and dashed off the new story, with its chillingly controlled climax, in a flurry of activity. Its defining image, that of Ligeia returned to some form of life from beyond the grave, appearing with her grave cerements still about her and still apparently uncorrupted, is perhaps one reason why readers of *Pym* see the shrouded phantom there as female in form. It is possible that in both texts Poe was also thinking of the "nightmare Death-in-Life" in *The Rime of the Ancient Mariner* by Samuel Taylor Coleridge, for whom Poe expressed a qualified admiration but with whom he had much in common thematically and prosodically.

It is perhaps ironic that having escaped Baltimore, Poe should find a ready market there. He also sold a poem to the *Museum*; "The Haunted Palace", another attempt to symbolise moral and psychological decadence through the decline of a great building, became one of the building blocks of another great story, "The Fall of the House of Usher". In November 1838, the same magazine published a pastiche horror story "The Scythe of Time" and a related piece called "The Psyche Zenobia", later better known as "How to Write a Blackwood Article" when it was published as such in *Phantasy Pieces,* and interesting for what it tells us about his literary values at the time.

Poe understood the power and the very particular Americanness of magazines. He was obviously well aware of the Edinburgh-based *Blackwood's Magazine,* and the kind of thoughtful writing and criticism associated with it. (*Blackwood's* published one of the more sober reviews of Poe's *Tales* in 1845.) It was the kind of thing he aspired to and perhaps hoped to find in Philadelphia, away from the circulation-chasing New York press. It is ironic that during his first year there, Poe published little in the Pennsylvania magazines, even the one run by his old contact, Mrs Hale. Poe's detestation of "the mob" was in part political, in large measure aesthetic. While he knew better than anyone at the time what might make a saleable story or poem, even prided himself on knowing the formula, he hankered after a more high-minded approach to creative writing and its public reception. That is what threw him up against William E. Burton and his magazine; what led him to write his brave manifesto for the stillborn *Penn Magazine*; and what ultimately, through need and compromise, to his highest achievement as an editor, at *Graham's.*

7

"Ill-conceived and miserably executed": Poe as editor and critic, 1839–42

The six years he spent in Philadelphia marked the pinnacle of Poe's professional success, his achievement as a writer, and possibly his personal happiness as well. Most of the great stories by which he is known were published at this time, as well as founding work in American literary criticism, work far more perspicacious, generous and even-handed than its anatagonistic reputation might suggest. In Philadelphia he began to rub shoulders with his literary peers, including the visiting Charles Dickens, whose "Boz" sketches he had reviewed favourably in the *Messenger*, when Dickens was still unknown in America, and only beginning to carve a reputation at home. The respect was mutual, if somewhat chastened on Dickens' part. There is a story that simply by reading the opening instalments, Poe was able to predict the ending of *Barnaby Rudge*, prompting Dickens to say "The devil's in the man". Given that Poe and Dickens met in Philadelphia in March 1842 and Dickens' historical novel ran in his magazine *Master Humphrey's Clock* in 1840 and 1841, there are some problems with the anecdote, but it adds another attractive frisson to the notion of Poe as a man of unearthly powers. In reality, the "prediction" ran in a review Poe contributed to the *Saturday Evening Post*; and while he was correct about some details, such as identifying Rudge as a murderer, he was quite wrong in others.

There were clouds on the family horizons even amidst success. Sometime in 1839, Poe moved Virginia and Mrs Clemm from a small house on Sixteenth Street to the more attractive Fairmount area, apparently because of concerns over Virginia's health. Three years later, it broke down entirely, beginning the long, slow death-in-life of the consumptive, which must have seemed as if "Ligeia" had come back to haunt Poe. Even if the magazines were beginning to pay for work, money was still a constant worry (Dickens later offered financial help to Mrs Clemm) and during his time in Philadelphia Poe undertook the strangest piece of hack-work of his career. Published "for the author" by Haswell, Barrington and Haswell, *The Conchologist's First Book: or A System of Testaceous Conchology, etc* was, ironically, the only book bearing Poe's name that went into a second edition during his lifetime. Whether he was in any sense the author was immediately questioned. The charge of plagiarism seems well-founded, since much of the text was lifted without change from a textbook published in Glasgow less than a decade before and from a monography on conchology published even more recently in the United States by a Professor Thomas Wyatt. Some have fancifully argued that Poe, with his omnivorous curiosity and fascination with all branches of science, had contracted an interest in the subject while a serving soldier at Sullivan's Island, and he does seem to have had enthusiastic conversations with a Dr Ravenel who had also lived and studied there. Even so, his claims on authorship are slender and his affronted rejection of the plagiarism charge not entirely consistent. However, it does seem that Wyatt (possibly with a Professor McMurtrie) approached Poe with a request for a cheap, schools edition of his *magnum opus* and persuaded the rising star to put his name to it as a way of drumming up sales. Poe also seems to have used his fluency in French to translate taxonomical descriptions from Cuvier. Whatever the truth, it remains the oddest item in the Poe bibliography, more significant for the poignant way it bespeaks a need for any work that paid a fee or honorarium, even if it was only for the use of his name.

The name was now well enough known for Poe to be able to trade on it. He made contact with William E. Burton and offered his services to the *Gentleman's Magazine (American Monthly Review)* which Burton, an English-born actor who still had ambitions in the theatre, had founded in Philadelphia two years earlier. On May 11 1839, Burton wrote back offering Poe $10 per week in return for two hours a day of editorial work. It is a friendly, but cautious letter, which ends almost off-handedly with "I shall dine at home today at 3. If you will cut your mutton with me, good. If not, write or see me at your leisure". It seems that Poe may have chosen the latter option and to ignore Burton's careful enumeration of the magazine's financial problems and insufficient circulation, because a later reply from Burton exists that suggests Poe may have sent off one of his hectoring pleas or unsolicited lectures about the magazine business. Burton expresses regret at the young man's woes, but with some impatience, too: "I am sorry that you thought necessary to send me such a letter as your last. The troubles of the world have given a morbid tone to your feelings which it is your duty to discourage... . I have been as severely handled in the world as you can possibly have been, but my sufferings have not tinged my mind with a melancholy hue, nor do I allow my views of my fellow creatures to be jaundiced by the fogs of my own creation".

The letter is notorious because after Poe's death, his obituarist and executor Rufus Griswold rewrote passages in it – the autograph still exists, so there is no doubt of this – to suggest that Poe had proposed a new, sensationalist approach for the magazine, and may even have insulted Burton in the process. Griswold's motivation may become clearer later, but the real reply is firm but kindly. Burton does not say "I will gladly overlook the past" (which strongly implies some offence given and taken) but he does suggest that they should meet as if the correspondence had not taken place.

Whatever was said or done seems to have been quickly because by June Poe's appointment was noted in the magazine and by the following volume he was listed along with Burton as an editor. He clearly wanted to make an early mark for among the many reviews Poe contributed to the three summer issues of the *Gentleman's Magazine* is a notably vicious account of James Fenimore Cooper's *A History of the United States Navy*. Though hardly qualified to pass comment on the subject, Poe used the occasion to launch an attach on Cooper's "Leatherstocking Tales" which he dismissed as "a flashy succession of ill-conceived and miserably executed literary productions, each more silly than its predecessor". Unlike Poe, who merely dreamed of it, Cooper really had gone to sea, albeit briefly, resigning his naval commission in 1811. The review did, however, look like kicking a man when he was down. The "Leatherstocking" series, whose prose and politics could not possibly have appealed to Poe, had rather stalled after *The Last of the Mohicans* and *The Prairie*, partly because Cooper travelled widely in those years, testing his own republicanism against European political models, largely because he had become so embroiled in controversy and litigation with a hostile press that fiction writing was sidelined. A year after his naval history, a more worthy piece of journey-work than Poe's conchological treatise, Cooper returned with *The Pathfinder* and *The Deerslayer*, which concluded the sequence in that decrescendo of reality D. H. Lawrence so much admired.

Poe was flexing his muscles, but also firing the first shots in what was to become a long campaign of literary provocation that saw him become an able controversialist and the implacable foe of such sanctified figures as Henry Wadworth Longfellow. It might also seem that in writing like this, stridently, *ad hominem*, always going for the jugular, he went against not only Burton's dislike of sensation but also the tone of high seriousness and literary purity that he dreamed of for his own never-to-be-realised magazine project. Poe was not writing – or publishing – very much poetry at this time and the few things he published in Burton's magazine were dismissed as "odds and ends ... to fill out a vacancy left at the foot of a prose article". Nor did he show much inclination to sustain his experiment with novel-writing. Though some have expressed doubts as to Poe's authorship, he did produce several instalments of a long narrative called "The Journal of Julius Rodman, being an account of the First Passage across the Rocky Mountains of North America ever achieved by Civilized Man". There is good reason why Poe's admirers have questioned his hand in it, because "Poe's unfinished novel" is a drably generic tale, taking its tone and much of its detail from a number of recent travelogues, and notably John K. Townsend's account of a journey across the Rockies. Significantly, the story simply came to an abrupt halt when Poe parted company from Burton in the summer of 1840; had it mattered to him, and had *Pym* received a warmer welcome, Poe would presumably have finished it.

In subordinating poetry to prose and the novel to the short story as a form, Poe may have sensed a shift in public taste; perhaps his own muse had changed dress. In November 1840, he saw his first collection of stories published in two volumes by Lea & Blanchard of Philadelphia, on severely disadvantageous terms that saw him signing away any potential profit in return for twenty copies to give friends. (The book was dedicated to Judge William Drayton, who may have contributed to production costs.) Its title, *Tales of the Grotesque and Arabesque,* implies a certain distinction between two kinds of story. Poe had borrowed the terms from Sir Walter Scott, and though he uses them fairly casually (and inconsistently), they seem to fall pretty much in line with the Coleridgean dichotomy of "fancy" and "imagination". Poe's grotesques are mainly lightweight satires and caprices, his arabesques the more profoundly conceived and psychological of the stories. The terms originally applied to styles of decoration in Islamic architecture and design and given his lifelong fascination with all things Oriental and Levantine, it can be assumed that Poe knew that; in May 1840, he used "arabesque" in its proper context in "The Philosophy of Furniture", one of his last essays for the *Gentleman's Magazine.*

Precise definitions of form mattered rather less to him than how universally the stories would be understood. Already a shrewd observer and manipulator of the literary scene, Poe knew to get his retaliation in first. His famous preface to the *Tales* anticipates the criticism that his stories are too dependent on European models, and specifically Germanic ones. "If in many of my productions terror has been the thesis, I maintain that terror is not of Germany but of the soul".

Of the twenty-five tales collected, all except one minor piece ("Why the Little Frenchman Wears His Hand In A Sling") had been published before. Though Poe had managed to place some stories elsewhere, and would continue to sell stories to Christmas annuals over the next few years, Burton and his magazine were the main beneficiaries. In August 1839, he published "The Man That Was Used Up – A Tale of the Late Bugaboo and Kickapoo Campaign". At first glance, this is a skimpy satire, but the story of an old general who has lost so many body parts that he is more prosthetic than living tissue has a decidedly modern, or modernist, cast and may very well have exerted an influence on the Nathanael West's 1934 novel *A Cool Million: The Dismantling of Lemuel Pitkin*, which satirises the "Horatio Alger" myth of self-improvement. Though Poe's story sits unmistakably among the "grotesques", its underlying theme – how much of a human being must remain to preserve the integrity of the self – is not so very different to that of one of his best and most famous stories, also included among the *Tales*.

As described in chapter three, "William Wilson" drew something from Poe's schooldays in London. At the simplest level, it is a classic *doppelganger* story, but its philosophical subtlety clinches Poe's determination to locate moral terror in the soul, and thus a universal quality, rather than in literary convention. Wilson's double, it becomes clear, is his own moral nature, which is to say something more than a Disneyish "conscience", whose separate existence leaves Wilson reduced to mere sentience and appetites. Inevitably, he comes to resent the presence of the other Wilson and kills him, discovering in the process that he has destroyed himself. The climax, and its attendant moral, are familiar enough to audiences raised on Robert Louis Stevenson and *Dr Jekyll and Mr*

Hyde or, still more, James Hogg's *Confessions of a Justified Sinner,* but what is distinctive about Poe's story is the way he builds and sustains tension by subtle association, carefully occluded detail and by the simple cadence of his sentences. The story's autobiographical dimension seems to have troubled Poe enough to wish to blur it. His narrator states that "my namesake was born on the nineteenth of January … . – and this is precisely the day of my own [and Edgar Allan Poe's!] nativity"; only in the *Tales* is the year given as 1809; in other versions, as first published in *The Gift,* and then in Burton's magazine, it is given as either 1811 or 1813. As with *Pym,* the connections between character and creator are teasingly offered and then withdrawn.

What is additionally striking about "William Wilson" is that the central character's dominant quality, and the source of his moral "justification", is a hypertrophic imagination or overdevelopment of the aesthetic side. This is very much in line with the qualities later attributed by Robert Louis Stevenson to his Mr Hyde, who is not "evil" in an easy or obvious sense but rather an expression of imaginings more extreme than those of ordinary humanity. Something of the same emerges in another of Poe's very greatest stories, also published among the *Tales.* "The Fall of the House of Usher" finds the nameless narrator drawn by the call of friendship to visit Roderick Usher, a man in whom the senses – auditory, visual, olfactory – are so heightened as to border on madness. He lives in an artificially occluded environment designed to protect him from painful sensation. This is at some level a projection of Poe himself, who feared that his own openness to sensation would lead inexorably to madness. As if to confirm the autobiographical dimension, Poe reprints his poem "The Haunted Palace" within the story, but attributes it to Usher. In these verses Poe had brilliantly communicated by subtle slippages of metre the drift of an orderly and happy family living under the protection of God towards a howling insanity – the same effect might have been achieved by introducing non-functional discords and displaced beats in otherwise conventional music – but as in the earlier "The City in the Sea", his aim was to suggest a fateful unity between spiritual decadence and the physical environment. "The Fall of the House of Usher" also shares some signature devices with the poem about the doomed city, not least a certain mysterious quality of light-without-source, which in the poem seems to point to some hellish conflagration brewing below but in the story seems more like the glow that comes off rotting wood or flesh.

There is a further dimension to Roderick Usher's spiritual crisis. He lives with his twin sister Madeline whose apparent death after the visitor's arrival and disruption of the siblings' precariously shared identity leads to the now familiar trope of premature entombment. For a brief time, Roderick is singular but in his singularity spiritually meaningless. When Madeline subsequently dies, his identity and that of his "house" is snuffed out and as the narrator flees the building that has both contained and expressed the brother and sister succumbs to the cracks that have been steadily widening in its structure and collapses into the dark waters of the lake that surrounds it. Much is bound up in this story: contemporary fears of congenital madness and of inherited disease like syphilis or the tuberculosis that would shortly come to haunt the Poes. However, its central theme remains the search for some understanding of what demarcates a human self. Like all great writers, Poe is an obsessive, harping constantly on a single string which then in turn makes all other human concerns resonate, for if the self cannot confidently be defined what hope is there of understanding love, or politics?

Even before the book publication of the *Tales*, Poe was politicking strongly on his own behalf, writing to friends and literary men in the hope of good reviews, but also firing some first, unseemly shots in what would be a long campaign against Henry Wadsworth Longfellow, who he admired above all other American poets, aside from Lowell and, implicitly himself; Poe always intended to get back to verse. (Shortly thereafter, in his next editorial role, Poe was writing to Longfellow in markedly sycophantic and self-denying terms, requesting literary contributions and offering "*carte blanche*" in respect of terms, and was doubtless mollified to have the older poet reply that, far from never having heard of Poe, Longfellow already had a "high idea of your power". Such, though, is literary politics: much noise and antagonism on the surface; respect, however grudging, beneath.) Self-promotion and literary skirmishing are as old as the classical world and have not died out in modern times, though perhaps they are now practised more circumspectly. There is little to choose between a contemporary apparatus of agents, advertising, personal appearances, singings and book festivals and a 19th century author's attempts to advance his own work; though by our recent standards Walt Whitman's glowing review of his own *Leaves of Grass* seems underhand and fraudulent, such a manoeuvre would have been perfectly familiar to those few at the time who understood how the publishing business worked behind the scenes. And Edgar Allan Poe, who could expect no further financial gain from his stories, even those few which might be republished in another journal, had an acute and immediate need to sell his name and reputation.

Just as the tropes of his work are becoming familiar, so

too are the tropes of his life. His separation from Burton is marked by the same mix of ambiguity, mutual recrimination, rumours of vice, hasty speech and underlying ambition, all tempered by what seems to have been genuine affection and respect. That Poe exceeded his quota of work for Burton is not in doubt; much unsigned copy in the magazine can confidently be attributed to him and in a letter to his employer, impetuously drafted and perhaps not sent, he claims to have written 132 pages between July 1839 and June 1840. The latter date marks his break with Burton, though the exact reason remains uncertain. Poe was certainly aware that he was being accused of drunkenness. In another letter, written almost a year after he left the *Gentleman's Magazine* and already cited in chapter , he admits to an episode of intoxication while at the *Messenger*, but to all intents and purposes claims to be teetotal. Most who knew him at the time remember a hardworking man of gentle character and unfailing generosity. This, of course, excludes those who found themselves the object of his critical barbs, and as a "character" of Poe fails to account for the usual combination of hurt, insult and obsessive detail found in that possibly unsent letter to Burton: he calls his employer an "ass", accuses him of bullying, reminds him of a bad review of *Pym* (albeit dismissed by its author in the same sentence as "a very silly book"), pleads poverty, complains of ungenerosity (while admitting that Burton granted loans and advances on salary), and then obsessively itemises other duties done and monies owed on both sides. Set it alongside one of the many letters written to John Allan a decade earlier and the tone and import is disturbingly similar.

Burton had put his magazine up for sale, apparently without telling Poe. He was losing money that would have preferred to invest in his new "National" theatre, and he seemed disinclined to fight his way out of problems. In Poe's *de facto* letter of resignation, he rather lamely threatens Burton with a premature end to "Julius Rodman", to which he had shown no real commitment even in the early stages, but more significantly, and with utter bad faith, claims that had it not been for Burton's decision to pull out of the magazine, he – Poe – would never have "dreamed of attempting one of my own".

In reality, it had been a dream for some considerable time, and would remain an obsessive one for the rest of Poe's life. The aim was to publish a magazine of high literary merit and exacting production standards, free of "any tincture of the profanity, scurrility, or profanity, which are the blemish of some of the most vigorous of the European prints", but modelled somewhat on *The Knickerbocker* and the *North American Review*; inevitably expensive, but cast in new – rather than once-used and blurry – type; its aim chiefly to "*please*" rather than to educate or comment on current affairs and matters of high philosophical concern.

In a prospectus, printed up in ambitious quantities in the summer of 1840 and subsequently used reversed for business and personal correspondence, Poe makes it clear that his aim is for national coverage, a universal rather than parochial perspective, and the very best of American writers – he later mentions Longfellow, Cooper, William Cullen Bryant and Washington Irving with the airy confidence of a man who has somehow already secured their services – but interestingly his main appeal for support went out "to the many thousands of my friends, and especially of my Southern friends, who sustained me in the Messenger, where I had but a very partial opportunity of completing my own plans". It seems certain that the desire to edit and publish a magazine of his own did indeed go back to Baltimore days. Significantly, he makes no mention of recent employment at *Burton's*.

The original plan was to launch his "Penn Magazine" on January 1 1841, but illness and other circumstances forced a postponement. By that summer, Poe had once again put off the launch to the start of 1842, and was no longer speaking about a solo venture, but instead collaboration with a Mr Graham. In reality, Poe was once again an employee, though this time apparently a successful one. His dreams of launching the "Penn" as an up-market adjunct to *Graham's* quickly lost the tinge of reality, but because dreams are more infinitely malleable than actual projects Poe never ceased to believe that his unpublished magazine, later re-named "The Stylus", had been denied an inevitable success. The deal struck with Mr Graham had delivered a salary, but lost Poe his self-promised moment of individual glory; his perceived success with *Graham's* had, he believed, lost himself as much money as he had made for its proprietor. It must have rankled to find himself on a fixed income, with supernumerary payments only for exceptional work, while Graham paid generously for freelance contributions from Poe's literary rivals. As so often, though, the facts speak differently. For a start, Poe's duties were relatively light, much of the drudge-work on the magazine being left to a Mr Peterson and to two female editors subsequently taken on. By the same token, while it is usually claimed that Poe alone or largely was responsible for the magazine's success, the magical circulation figure of 40,000 was only reached six months after he had left *Graham's* and almost certainly for reasons unconnected to Poe's writing.

Even before he was properly launched at *Graham's*, Poe was looking at possibilities elsewhere, even outside publishing. A recent friend, Frederick W. Thomas (who seems also to have known the unhappy Henry) suggested that Poe might find a minor post in government; the steady growth of "big government" in the US, exponential under the administrations of Tyler, meant there were sinecures to be had. Almost every other significant American writer of the period had some kind of public or academic post to support their literary endeavours, but Poe never enjoyed such a safety net. As he poignantly wrote to Thomas, "To coin one's brain into silver, at the nod of a master, is to my thinking, the hardest task in the world". How much easier he would have found it to answer to a political master is hard to gauge, but neither Poe's personality nor his Whig politics would have helped him much at this juncture. John Pendleton Kennedy was a congressman but presumably too busy, too cautious or too chastened by past events to recommend Poe for anything. As for the 32-year-old applicant, he perhaps set too much store on a brief and now distant cadetship at West Point to bring him to the notice of either president or secretary of war.

Things could have been worse. From the start and for all his misgivings and thwarted ambitions, he seems to have enjoyed a warm and intelligent relationship with his new proprietor, who was as warm as he was punctilious in business, George Rex Graham was younger than Poe, just 27, but had shown resolve and enterprise in his young life, paying his bills as a carpenter, working as an editorial assistant and proofreader on a number of Philadelphia papers, even buying out one of them. At the end of 1840, he acquired the *Gentleman's Magazine* from Burton, paying a shrewd $1 per existing subscriber. It isn't clear, since we only have Poe's version of events, whether plans for the *Penn* to publish in tandem were ever actual or realistic, or simply a pipe-dream. Seeing his circulation climb even upwards and the literary quality of his magazine steadily increase, Graham might have been inclined to give the older man his head, or he might just as reasonably have wanted to keep him applied to more realistic and lucrative concerns.

If Burton and others got some of the finest of Poe's stories, any concern about burn-out after the commercial stillbirth of the *Tales* was quickly allayed. Some of the very finest were still to come, and Graham had the luck to begin with one of the most presciently modern. In the December 1840 issue, even before Poe's editorial role had been formalised – he officially joined the magazine in April – *Graham's* published "The Man of the Crowd". Though it lacks the usual apparatus of terror, it works at a much deeper level, conveying a sense of object-less anxiety in an individual who fears his own thoughts sufficiently to seek the anonymous solace of the mass, prowling the streets of London, pursued by the curious narrator who seems to recognise in the elderly figure some human archetype of modernity. One only needs to look forward a century to the early works of Saul Bellow to recognise a similar imagination at work and a similar sense of identity in crisis.

Poe's own fear of the undifferentiated "democratic" mass is clearly at work here and it is reflected, too, in his feelings about the magazine that employed him. George Graham's own taste, or his market-sense, ran to the populist and sentimental. He had briefly owned the middle-brow *Casket*, after all. When Poe complained to Frederick Thomas of the "namby-pamby" cast of *Graham's* pages, he may well have been acknowledging the unwelcome conclusion that it was, indeed, the "contemptible pictures, fashion-plates, music and love-tales" that had stoked the subscription list, and not his high-minded prose.

Almost at the end of his time with *Graham's*, Poe published a review of Nathaniel Hawthorne's *Twice-Told Tales* which, in addition to violating somewhat his complaint elsewhere that reviewers were prone to discussing not so much the book in hand as its subject, gives away something of himself. It also suggests that while he continued to write prose rather more than poetry, he still regarded the rhymed poem of relatively short duration as the highest expression of literary art. The same basic principle, though, applies to the short story. He explains: "A skilful literary artist has constructed a tale. If wise, he has not fashioned his thoughts to accommodate his incidents; but having conceived, with deliberate care, a certain unique or single *effect* to be wrought out, he then invents such incidents – he then combines such events as may best aid him in establishing this preconceived effect". This was precisely the method employed some years later to write "The Raven", perhaps his most celebrated creation and one of his most durable.

In the application of the intellect, the truly creative genius distinguished himself from the herd of entertainers. Much of Poe's writing for *Graham's* has a similar subtext. His story "A Descent into the Maelstrom", published in May 1841, purports to correct prevailing thought about the creation of whirlpools. In his prose poem "The Isle of the Fay", which was headed in the June 1841 issue with a reworked version of the sonnet "To Science", Poe seems to offer an untypical celebration of nature unmediated by the intellect, except that he makes it clear that landscape and natural grandeur are really artefacts of the mind's totalising function, which dislikes disorder and marshals all experience *sub specie aeternitatis*. It is useful to compare this approach to that of Ralph Waldo Emerson, one of the writers Poe spoke of critically elsewhere in *Graham's,* and his theories of Nature and the "Oversoul".

His devotion to the intellect better coincided with his

instincts as both journalist and entertainer in another article and story of the period. In 1839, Poe had contributed a piece to *Alexander's Weekly Messenger* in Philadelphia called "Enigmatical and Conundrum-ical", in which he offered to solve any cryptogram sent in by readers. He picked up the idea again in "A Few Words on Secret Writing" for *Graham's*, in which he claimed to have solved 99 out of the one hundred puzzles sent in by readers (the other one he declared unsolvable) and to have even solved cryptograms based on foreign key-words from modern and classical languages. Something of the same spirit informs his famous story "The Murders in the Rue Morgue", published in April 1841. Poe called it a tale of ratiocination; it is now often regarded as the first modern detective story.

Its originality lies less in the actual elements of the narrative than in their extraordinary compression. He borrows the name of his fictional detective C. Auguste Dupin from a story about the French police minister Vidocq serialised in *Burton's* three years before, though again, like Arthur Gordon Pym, its cadence immediately recalls "Edgar Allan Poe". He remembered the Dubourg sisters who ran the little dame-school in London, and gave the name to one of the witnesses at the inquest. The orang-utang who actually commits the grisly murder of Mme and Mlle L'Espanaye is seemingly borrowed from Sir Walter Scott's *Count Robert of Paris*. Nevertheless, Poe lays his trail in a highly original way, setting out false clues and motivations which point to murder in the course of robbery, and incidentally dismissing the skills of Vidocq as mere guesswork and luck. It is only by analysing all the available facts and exploring the curious detail of the two voices heard at the scene, one speaking French, one an unknown tongue, that Dupin arrives at the conclusion that the perpetrator is not only foreign but not even human. The conclusion is as morally intriguing as it is virtuosic.

Between November 1841 and January 1842, Poe published a short series of articles that cleverly combined entertainment with serious literary thought. "A Chapter on Autography" purports to give the characters of around 100 American literary men based on their autograph responses to a wholly imaginary letter. At one level this is little more than an *esprit*, similar in tone if not approach to the "Henry Root" letters that showed off the great and good to some personal disadvantage in the British press of the 1970s. At another, it is more like Norman Mailer's notorious "Quick Glance at the Talent in the Room", a series of short literary portraits originally written for the *Village Voice* and subsequently republished in his *Advertisements for Myself*. What is interesting about Poe's pieces is similar to what is interesting in Mailer's: early and subjective impressions of writers who were later to become important; glimpses of figures important at the time who have since sunk into obscurity; and insight into friendships and feuds. Lowell and Longfellow are again praised, though Poe is at this stage unwilling to concede absolute precedence in verse to anyone; Emerson is rather dismissed; others, mostly newspaper editors and magazine men, are delivered barbed comments which can only be explained on the basis of past slights and professional rivalry.

One, however, stands out: a 26-year-old poet, editor and Baptist clergyman whom Poe had met in the spring of 1841 and described six months later as "a gentleman of fine taste and sound judgement". He was the Rev Rufus Wilmot Griswold, whose "taste, talent, and *tact*" (a later, still more ironic judgement) would soon be put aside in the sole interest of destroying Poe's reputation for ever. For the moment, though, a more immediate and personal nemesis was looming.

8

"Long intervals of horrible sanity": Poe's short stories, 1842–44

In January 1842, Virginia Poe suffered a sudden haemorrhage while singing at her piano. For a time, it seemed as if she would not recover and the house at Coates Street stood for many weeks in a state of anxiety that hovered close to mourning.

It is not clear whether Virginia's health had been causing concern before the attack. "Eleanora", published in *The Gift* in late 1841, is a revealing story of the period, working a gentler variation on the familiar Morella/Ligeia pattern. According to the sentimental pattern, the beautiful Eleanora seems too fine for this world and succumbs to illness. Her dying fear – and the relocation of dread is a key element in this version – is that her husband will forget her. He pledges his love for eternity, but does eventually remarry, and in a waking dream hears Eleanora's voice giving her blessing and setting him free.

Compare this oddly complacent and rationalising tale, which might well have been written to reassure both an ailing wife and a guilt-ridden husband, with another, published some months after Virginia's first attack. "Life in Death", an almost stereotypically "Poe" title later changed to "The Oval Portrait", tells how a wounded man takes refuge in a castle and finds a disturbingly life-like portrait of a beautiful girl. An old book nearby explains that as she sat to her artist husband, the girl's life was steadily taken from her and transferred to canvas. In retrospect, it seems a hackneyed theme, reworked in various forms by Oscar Wilde and Roald Dahl, and more contemporaneously with Poe by Nathaniel Hawthorne in "The Birthmark", but one cannot deny Poe his originality.

Death stalked another of the stories published that spring, again in *Graham's*. Of all the Poe tales later adapted for film by Roger Corman and others, "The Masque of the Red Death" seems most "cinematic" in conception, marked by intense, saturated colours that symbolise different spiritual states. Inside Prince Prospero's luxuriously appointed Abbey all is beauty and pleasure; "The external world could take of itself. In the meantime, it was folly to grieve, or to think". The external world has, of course, succumbed to the plague, but the fragile barrier between inner and outer, life and death, beauty and horror has been breached by the figure of the Red Death, who stalks the rich rooms in search of the hedonistic Prince and his guests, touching none but spreading an atmosphere of guilty dread. Poe's chief gift here lies in the scene-setting, but what makes the tale powerful is the absence of any clear conclusion. When the revellers find their courage and attack the spectral figure, they find nothing but empty grave-cloths, spattered with blood but animated by nothing other than a dark moral intent too troubling for these pleasure-seekers. With the coming of HIV/AIDS, the tale acquired a new and sometimes awkward aura of significance – senseless pleasure followed by punishment, a connection and blood and contagion – which was no part of Poe's original intention. In sustained atmosphere and unity of effect, it is among the most virtuosic of all his works, but it must also have been tinged by his fears for Virginia, and for himself.

A question is posed in "Eleanora": whether "madness is or is not the loftiest intelligence – whether much that is glorious, whether all that is profound – does not spring from disease of thought – from moods of mind, exalted at the expense of the general intellect". This was the Poe admired by the French Symbolists, who elevated irrationality above reason, and found creative value in disease rather than balance. But Poe was thinking first and foremost of his own situation. Virginia had a further attack later in the year, and they came again and again until she died five summers later. The effect on Poe was drastic. Those who later defended his reputation against Griswold's attacks always mentioned not just the devoted and loving atmosphere of the little house they had visited but also Poe's dedication to hard work. This latter was as much the problem as Virginia's decline. Work drove Poe, but also drove him mad. A year before he died he recalled a constitutional sensitivity and nervousness. "I became insane, with long intervals of horrible sanity" – and how chilling a formulation that is – "During these fits of absolute unconsciousness I drank, God only knows how often or how much. As a matter of course my enemies referred the insanity to the drink rather than the drink to the insanity". This is the usual mix of painful self-knowledge and further rationalisation; drinking while absolutely unconscious somewhat absolves the drinker. There seems no reason to doubt that these attacks were in large part influenced by Virginia's health and the emotional roller-coaster of hopeful remissions followed by worrying declines. Poe's devotion is undoubted.

When he died, Graham recalled a "rapturous worship" of Virginia, heightened by the imminence of loss, and was in no doubt that the daily strain of watching her decline contributed materially to Poe's problems.

The split with Graham may well have been hastened by his drinking, though Graham himself was too kindly and tactful a soul to make any reference to it. Hovering before Poe, though, was not only the fading image of Virginia but also that of his beloved journal project. Again, he chafed at working for someone else's profit and according to someone else's middlebrow editorial principles.

The July 1842 issue of *Graham's* included a brief notice offering good wishes to Poe in his future endeavours; he had apparently left two months earlier, but in correspondence of the time hints that he might be re-engaged and set about ridding *Graham's* of "quackery". Elsewhere, though, his thoughts run in different directions: to the possibility of a new collaborative magazine with an unidentified "Foster" in New York; and to the publication of a new collection of stories. One might expect the motive this time to be profit, but as early as August 1841 Poe was offering Lea & Blanchard a second, enlarged edition but on the same no-profit terms as the first. They briskly declined, on the quite understandable grounds that stocks of the original collection were still far from exhausted. A year later, Poe was still making plans for a volume which he now called *Phantasy-Pieces*. With boyish enthusiasm, he even sketched out a possible title page, written in his tidier, "print" hand and complete with an epigraph from Goethe. The only sign realistic touch comes at the bottom, where "Three Volumes" has been amended to "Two". More interesting, though, is what, in the summer of 1842, Poe thought to leave out of what was essentially a complete fictional prose. The autograph lists contains both new stories and old. Some of these have been revised and renamed: "The Homocamelopard" began life as "Epimanes" and "Four Beasts" in one, a slight satire on the credulous (Syrian, in name only) mob who turn on the king they worship when he appears dressed in animal skins. A similar skit, "Hans Phaal, a Tale" had appeared in the *Southern Literary Messenger* as early as summer 1835, intended as a hoax on the extravagantly overwritten stories of scientific expedition – in this case, to the moon – that were all the rage at the time. Poe has merely changed the title to "The Unparalleled Adventure of one Hans Pfaal". Oddly, he originally included two good new stories, surely essential to making any new volume marketable, and then deleted them. Published between November 1842 and February 1843 in "The Murder of Marie Roget" was based on a real life case; the luckless Mary Cecilia Rogers of New York was imaginatively transported to Paris in order that Auguste Dupin, now emerging as the world's first "series detective", might apply his powers of ratiocination to the case as he had in "The Murders in the Rue Morgue". Poe makes it clear in subsequent correspondence that his aim is not so much entertaining fiction or indeed a solution to the case as a more satisfactory approach to the known facts than the one advanced in the gutter press, which suggested gang involvement. Poe considered the death to have been accidental, following an illegal abortion; Mary's fiancé later killed himself at the same location, which suggests Poe may have been right.

His research wasn't quite so robust on the other story deleted from the proposed "Phantasy-Pieces" collection. Film critics have criticised Roger Corman's adaptation of "The Pit and The Pendulum" as bringing together too many extraneous elements. In truth, Poe himself stole ruthlessly from other sources and imported a Spanish Inquisition setting and sub-plot that has no historical veracity whatsoever. It's generally accepted that Poe took something of his plot from William Mudford's "The Iron Shroud", published (anonymously as by the author of "First and Last") in *Blackwood's Magazine* a dozen years before. The borrowing is of less significance than Poe's constant alertness to what was being published in Edinburgh and London. He also took elements from closer to home. Charles Brockden Brown's early American novel *Edgar Huntly* also plays with the idea of a young hero buried alive in a pit, though there is nothing there of Mudford's slowly closing walls or of Poe's vividly horrific swinging blade – half clock pendulum, half guillotine – which slowly descends on his protagonist's bound body.

If the image has obvious literary sources, it must also speak to Poe's own psychological state at the time, with the twin Damoclean swords of poverty and Virginia's ill health always above his head.

The story was written sometime in the spring or summer of 1842, when Poe again found himself desperate for funds. In one letter of the time he speaks of bankruptcy, almost as if a formal declaration of insolvency would relieve him of money concerns. In others, he admits to ill-health, much of it, reading between the lines, stress-induced. And as ever, he places undue and premature confidence in will o'the wisp employment schemes. Perhaps in emulation of Hawthorne, who had been working as a weigher and gauger in Boston, Poe had hopes of a job at the Philadelphia Custom House. Unlike the New Englander, who was a college friend of future president Franklin Pierce, Poe could only count on second-hand contacts with President John Tyler – whose son was a friend of a friend – and these came to nothing.

He did at least now have a circle of literary friends and a certain reputation as a man of letters. There can be some comfort in shared distress, but Poe does not seem to have been reassured – or warned – by the wreck of others' plans. While at *Graham's* Poe had struck up an admiring correspondence with James Russell Lowell and had published some of the younger man's poems. Some aspects of Lowell's life and character stand in sharp contrast to Poe's. Exactly a decade younger, he came through at a time when the economic shoals of American publishing were slowly becoming navigable by men of resource. And resourceful Lowell was, attaching himself to the cause of anti-slavery and writing regular columns for the London press on the subject. Where Poe politicked unrealistically for political office, Lowell had it fall into his lap, when in 1877 President Rutherford Hayes appointed him minister to the court of Spain. Even had Poe survived to the age of 60, it is hard to imagine any executive offering him such a role, especially after the portrayal of the Inquisition in "The Pit and the Pendulum".

Lowell may have had other advantages – not least a brilliantly gifted wife, the poet Maria White, who must have been contrasted sharply in Philadelphia's intellectual circles with the fey Virginia Poe – but he had his griefs to bear as well. As a young man, he'd suffered from a tendency to depression inherited from his mentally frail mother. The future was heavily mortgaged to sorrow and Lowell's immediate prospects were vulnerable to ill-health, but for the moment, as he recorded in *A Year's Life*, dedicated to Maria in 1841, he was looking resolutely forward. In the late summer of 1842, he announced the launch of a magazine *The Pioneer*. With more than a little hint of *quid pro quo,* though also with genuine admiration, Poe offered his services. Lowell accepted and in

January 1843 published "The Tell-Tale Heart", one of Poe's best psychological tales. He himself valued it on a par with "Ligeia", "The Murders in the Rue Morgue", "The Descent into the Maelstrom", "William Wilson" and "Usher", perhaps because best of all the tales it conveys a unity of mood, a palpable psychological reality in which the murderer really believes that he can hear the beating heart of his entombed victim and convinces the reader of the fact.

Poe was grateful for the promise of a $10 fee and for Lowell's show of confidence, but the appearance of *The Pioneer* only served to re-awaken his own dreams of the *Penn*. He set about re-launching the idea under better auspices and in January 1843 struck a deal with Thomas C. Clarke and Felix O. C. Darley that in exchange for editorial work on the Philadelphia *Saturday Museum*, or simply his now-bankable name on the masthead, they would underwrite what he was now calling in a new prospectus *The Stylus*. On the face of it, this arrangement sounds worryingly similar to the one supposedly struck with Graham; one wonders whether there really was a common understanding among the parties. For the moment, though, Poe's new partners were happy to (re)launch him as the coming man of American writing, throwing the emphasis again on his poetry, which was now substantially revised and quoting favourable references to him elsewhere as "one of the most powerful, chaste and erudite writers of the day". There is, however, also a reference to his "truly eventful life", which might suggest that Poe was still romancing, or at best blurring the line between fact and fiction in his work.

If the rhetoric was encouraging, the external auguries were not. Lowell's *Pioneer* closed after only three months, not because it had failed to recoup the initial investment (though there had barely been time for that) but because Lowell was struck down by serious eye disease. The closure left him nearly $2000 in debt and pushed him for a time away from the public eye, making him reclusive. He was obliged to write to Poe and apologise for non-payment.

Poe was having to write letters of apology on his own account. In the spring of 1843, he went to Washington, still hoping to lobby the White House for as position, but also to look for subscribers for *The Stylus*. His associations and opinions were too freely and unwisely expressed to win him any favour with "His Accidency" (Tyler had become acting president on the death of William Henry Harrison, and rules of succession were still not clear), a Southerner and "man without a party" whose personal politics led directly to the sectional politics of the next two decades. In addition, Poe seems to have succumbed to an old vice and disgraced himself while drunk. That his problem was clinical alcoholism rather than merely over-indulgence seemed increasingly clear; one friendly observer referred to the "Rubicon" of a single glass of wine or beer. In June, Poe writes to Lowell that "sickness and domestic affliction", as well as the "imbecility" and "idiocy" of his new business partner have left plans for *The Stylus* in pieces. Three months later, he writes again, asking if Lowell can, after all, send the $10 he is owed for "The Tell-Tale Heart". This time, the letter points to "domestic and pecuniary trouble" and alludes to a moment when Poe "nearly succumbed", though whether to ill-health or bankruptcy isn't entirely clear, even in the context of his request.

He could not quite let go of the magazine dream. Even in the spring of 1844, he was still talking about a high-quality $5 publication (as opposed to the usual $3 for a more commercial and popular offering) which would combine fine writing and serious criticism with – and this is the new obsession of a would-be editor who has twice fallen foul of unreliable or merely realistic partners – "Independence". A dream it was, and a dream it would remain. In the meantime, Poe was still obliged to hawk round his work. Though he sometimes gave the impression in correspondence that he could place work at will, the reality was less assured.

Even so, Poe had not entirely burned his bridges. *Graham's* was still publishing occasional pieces of his. In January 1843 the magazine had taken "The Conqueror Worm", a solitary new poem and a singularly untypical one which flails at its good-and-evil theme with un-Poe-like didacticism. Poe had also offered Graham a more typical piece, a puzzle-story about ciphers, maps and treasure called "The Gold Bug", but he recalled it in order to submit it for a $100 prize staked by the *Dollar Newspaper*, a broadsheet as far in style and quality from *Graham's*, *The Pioneer* or the still-born *Penn* and *Stylus* as might be imagined. He won the prize, and the story became a modest success, frequently reprinted and even dramatized at a downtown Philadelphia theatre.

"The Gold Bug" is a curious work. A beetle unknown to science becomes the clue to a huge cache of gold and jewels which seems to be associated with the notorious Captain Kidd. A crude cipher is also involved, and the work is an uneasy mix of confident naturalism – such as Poe's descriptions of Sullivan's Island, where the story is laid and where he was once posted as a soldier, awkward – and by present standards unseemly – caricature in the figure of the credulous black servant Jupiter, and some bewildering swerves of narrative logic.

Poe may well have wished at this time to devote more of his energies to writing verse, but the success of "The Gold Bug" (in May 1844, Poe claimed that, having sold the story on, there were 300,000 copies in circulation) must have convinced him anew that the public wanted tales instead. It would be another two years before he found a means to make money – and a national reputation – from poetry. For the moment, he returned to the idea of republishing his stories in a more permanent form. Once again, with the proposed *Phantasy Pieces* volume project rebuffed and still smarting from the bad deal struck with Lea & Blanchard for the *Tales*, he was obliged to trade down his ambitions and start issuing his stories in pamphlet form. That he refused to surrender entirely his high standards can be judged from the title given to the proposed series: "THE PROSE ROMANCES OF EDGAR A. POE". The idea was that at the modest price of eight numbers for a dollar, and with each number complete in itself, purchasers could build up a "UNIFORM SERIAL EDITION" of a writer intriguingly identified as author of "The Gold Bug", his best-received recent work, but also *Arthur Gordon Pym*, which Poe had dismissed as a "silly" book, and the unsuccessful *Tales of the Grotesque and Arabesque*. Poe obviously intended the series to follow the order he had chosen for the *Phantasy Pieces*, and revised the stories carefully. The publisher was William H. Graham of Chestnut Street, Philadelphia, no known relation of Poe's former employer George R. Graham, to whom he was having to repay the fee for his recalled story. The series began with "The Murders in the Rue Morgue" and "The Man Who Was Used Up". It also ended there as well, for the second number never appeared. Another dream thwarted.

Weighed down by family responsibilities, the sinister progress of Virginia's night-sweats, his own contentious relationship with the other literary men of Philadelphia, drinking when an empty purse wouldn't allow him to eat,

Poe had ample ground for unhappiness, even if he was its chief architect, and it is striking how often at this time he alludes to his time as a soldier at Sullivan's Island. His (very) scant knowledge of seashells was gained there and helped lend the (very) thinnest veneer of authority to his cobbled-together textbook. It is the setting for "The Gold-Bug" and would be the adventurer's landing place in his first successful story of 1844. By then, though, Poe and Virginia had gone from Philadelphia. It may have been hard to live there, but it was also hard to go, even though it is not clear what precisely prompted the decision. Though not quite an idyll, and though his greatest single success was still to come, it had been the scene of some of his very greatest work, and it had thrown up a few idyllic moments. Though we tend to think of Poe as a man of darkened interiors and of some self-seriousness, he sometimes opened himself to nature and sometimes let fall away – in print, as it clearly did in private – the air of intimidating authority he'd cultivated for so long. In a sketch sold to *The Opal* annual for 1844, he describes a drowsing afternoon in a skiff on the Wissahiccon [now Wissahickon] river near Philadelphia. The piece is a small and perhaps uncharacteristic plea for naturalness, for keeping the human touch and the utilitarian away from the great American interior. In a moment that might come from a James Fenimore Cooper novel, Poe spots a noble elk standing on a bluff. He has been day-dreaming about ancient times when there were no white faces in America and wonders whether the elk has been summoned up by imagination, "coupled with the red men of my vision". At that moment, a negro servant appears, holding out a piece of salt-lick. The "wild" creature approaches and then willingly kneels to be haltered. The animal is domesticated and belongs to an English family. It is a gentle, self-deprecating anecdote, but Quinn rightly gives it some prominence for it shows not only a different side of Poe's nature but also his unerring instinct for the way history ironises the most innocent moments: for here you have the myth of old, unexploited America, white settlement, the "peculiar institution" of slavery, the artist's romantic spectacles (short-sightedness was also the substance of a roughly contemporary story, slight but telling), all in one apparently throwaway passage. It's interesting that the tree that frames the scene is the tulip-poplar, the same *liriodendron tulipiferum* (Poe luxuriates in the taxonomical name) that provided the backdrop to his sun-warmed walks at Sullivan's Island. Perhaps he unconsciously hankered after those days: a secure billet; more hours of leisure, ironically enough, than now; orders taken and given in turn; a small but reliable wage; an order to life that the jobbing writer and impoverished freelance could only dream of; independence and space.

The "little house" was undoubtedly crowded and Poe seemed increasingly oppressed by the feuds he had sparked off and fanned in print. He had tried his luck in America's largest city seven years before and had been rebuffed. He perhaps forgot that he had made enemies there and that physical distance meant less in a world of rapidly developing mass communications. Whether born of foolish optimism or dictated by some undocumented disaster in Philadelphia, Poe was determined to give it another go. This time, with instructions to Mrs Clemm to stay behind for the moment and sell some books (unfortunately, some turned out not to be his for the selling), and with $11 in his pocket, he took Virginia to New York.

ooooo

"I have been roaming far and wide over this island of Man-nahatta ... (*why* do we persist in *de-euphonizing* the true names?) ... . Some portions of its interior have a certain air of rocky sterility which may impress some imaginations as simply *dreary* – to me it conveys the sublime. Trees are few: but some of the shrubbery is exceedingly picturesque." Thus Poe tried to reassure Pennsylvania readers – or himself – that the northern sojourn was going to be a happy one. He had already written to "Dear Muddy" to say that "Sis" had survived the sail north without coughs or fevers and was settled into a well-appointed boarding house at Greenwich Street; in point of fact, its nearness to the Hudson and its fogs could hardly have been beneficial for Virginia, but Poe seemed almost euphoric on first arrival and presents New York as a well-fed and easeful Cockaigne. Perhaps wisely, Poe quickly escaped the city proper and found lodgings with a family called Brennan who lived in one of the few surviving bucolic corners of Manhattan Island. It was there that he shortly wrote at least part of his most celebrated poem.

That first despatch south for the *Columbia Spy*, later reprinted in *Doings of Gotham*, strikes a characteristic note, pitched somewhere between boyish optimism (no tulip-pop-lars, but some very agreeable bushes) and arrogance; *you* might find this northern city desolate, it seems to say, whereas someone of my aesthetic sophistication is able to appreciate its grandeur. Yet the same series of letters contains a poign-ant reference, buried away in a review of poetry by his future defender Nathaniel Parker Willis. After a period in the United Kingdom, where his "Slingsby Papers" had offered British readers a glimpse of American life, Willis had returned to the US and to an idyllic patch of land on Oswego Creek in upstate New York. From there, though, he had been drawn back to the city as editor of the *New York Mirror*. Perhaps thinking more of himself and of that dreamy punt down the Wissahiccon, Poe sympathised with Willis's loss of "tranquillity and leisure … In his retirement he might have accomplished much, both for himself and for posterity; but, chained to the oar of a mere weekly paper, professedly addressing the frivolous and the fashionable, what can he now hope for but a gradual sinking into the slough of the Public Disregard?"

There seemed no immediate danger of the same thing happening to Poe. No longer a galley-slave to the weekly prints, Poe could sympathise with some complacency. In addition, within a week of his arrival he had managed to place a story with the *New York Sun* which by his own account had the newspaper's offices besieged with readers eager for an update on what was later known as "The Balloon-Hoax". The tale had originally been published under the headline "Astounding News by Express via Norfolk! THE ATLANTIC CROSSED N THREE DAYS, SIGNAL TRIUMPH OF MR. MONCK MASON'S FLYING MACHINE!"

Bizarrely, one of those who landed at Sullivan's Island from this (entirely fictitious) voyage in the steering balloon "Victoria" was given as Mr Harrison Ainsworth, author of *Jack Sheppard* and other successful tales. Ainsworth's presence on the passenger manifest and proxied postscript to the news report, plus Poe's characteristic detailing of the flight mechanisms, had apparently convinced much of New York that "The great problem is at length solved! The air, as well as the earth and the ocean, has been subdued by science, and will become a common and convenient highway for mankind." New York might also have smarted with envy that this great triumph should have been enjoyed in the South and not in the hub of progress.

Poe was securely launched by "The Balloon-Hoax". Even though he had alienated some of the most powerful editors in New York, he seemed to be having some success. Though he couldn't break down the doors of the *Knickerbocker* or melt the heart of its editor Lewis Gaylord Clark, he did manage to sell "The Oblong Box" to *Godey's*, where Mrs Hale, who'd known him for longer, was either more aware of Poe's marketability or more prepared to overlook past lapses. In July, the *Dollar Newspaper* published "The Premature Burial". A month later, the *Columbian Magazine* took "Mesmeric Revelation". Both stories make strong play of scientific accuracy, though after his imaginary transatlantic flight one wonders why anyone would regard Poe as a serious spokesman on current scientific thinking. Nevertheless, it obsessed him, and being in New York certainly put him closer to the most advanced scientific circles of the time, as well as a growing underswell of popular science and para-science in the magazines. It all led inexorably to *Eureka*, the strange scientific prose-poem that remains his most enigmatic and underrated work.

Poe was also hawking about another of his Dupin stories of ratiocination, "The Purloined Letter", but for the moment his attention seemed to have returned to verse, as it always did when the pressure of earning money eased and he could write from the heart rather than by the line. This time, though, Poe was able to combine critical appreciation with popular success. In the quiet of the Brennan house in semi-rural Mannahatta, he had been working on a poem that summed up not only his philosophy of prosodic composition but also his gift for atmosphere and evocative scene-setting. The poem was offered to Willis at the *Evening Mirror* and on January 29th 1845 it was published, with a short note from the publisher which declared it to be "unsurpassed in English poetry for subtle conception, masterly ingenuity of versification, and consistent sustaining of imaginative lift and 'pokerishness'" With admirable prescience and judgement, Willis added "It will stick to the memory of everybody who reads it."

9

"We peer into the abyss": Poe's decline, 1844–6

Almost all Americans know "The Raven". Most educated Americans also know something of how Poe claimed to have written it, for what might be the most ubiquitously anthologised and memorised verses of modern times – only a few Burns poems, "Hiawatha", and oddities like Joyce Kilmer's "Trees" come close – were also the subject of one of Poe's most notorious essays, "The Philosophy of Composition". Its notoriety lies less in the deliciously morbid suggestion that the death of a beautiful woman is "unquestionably the most poetical subject in the world" than in Poe's suggestion that poetry was somehow the product of entirely conscious, deliberate and logical procedures, all of them bearing on a clear conclusion and "unity of effect". Poe claimed to have written the climactic stanza of the poem first and to have fitted the other stanzas to it, making sure that none of them detracted from its impact. Like a cinematic *auteur,* he set his scene with very deliberate care: the night has to be stormy so the bird will be driven indoors; it perches "On the pallid bust of Pallas just above my chamber door", so that white marble or plaster will show up black plumage to best visual advantage, and imply in the process that this is no mere lover, but a learned lover. And so on: an assertion of complete control over every creative parameter.

The problem is that nobody knows how seriously "The Philosophy of Composition" was intended to be taken. So practised was Poe in the manipulation of his public that it is impossible to read the essay without sensing something of a put-on, or without catching just a tang of sarcasm. And yet, it is insufficient to dismiss the essay simply as a hoax, not least because for a century and a half a certain consensus understanding of how Poe wrote verse and constructed his prosody has been erected upon it. If he wrote with tongue in cheek, as many critics have suggested, he has been more widely believed, and unsceptically quoted, as not.

"The Philosophy of Composition" was first published in *Graham's* in April 1846, more than a year after "The Raven"'s public success. Though he republished it several times – "The bird beat the bug [i.e. "The Gold Bug"] all hollow" – he apparently received just $9 for the first publication of a poem that all of Eastern America was talking about. When he wrote his essay/manifesto Poe was struggling to keep his own magazine afloat: not *The Penn* or *The Stylus* of his dreams, but a less elevated publication to which he'd gained title and which he was struggling to keep afloat against the stern economic logic of American magazine publishing at the time, which meant that as long as US readers could subscribe to four or five British magazines, including the mighty *Blackwood's*, for less than Poe had been paid for his verses, why would they trouble with a more expensive home-grown press?

There is some bitterness behind "The Philosophy of Composition", but also a teasing approach to literary politics and theory. Poe makes a comradely gesture to his readers; unlike those writers who "positively shudder at letting the public take a peep behind the scenes", he is happy to explain how he goes about his work. In our present culture, almost pathologically obsessed with "making of ... "documentaries and demystifying biography, this is hardly unusual, but in a literary culture that had turned its back on classical models of creation based on craft, rules and conventions, it was an unusual tack indeed. By highlighting his own application of logic, pre-determined procedures for poetic creation, Poe was quite explicitly setting himself against a Romantic conception of poetry as "spontaneous creation"; Coleridge rising from a dream with "Kubla Khan" entire in his head (but fated to be unfinished because the real world intruded), the Boston Transcendentalists – or "Frogpondians" as Poe called them – in direct touch with Nature or the Oversoul.

There was a further barb to Poe's strictures, both personal and prescient. He was aware that most of the New England writers were clergymen, academics, holders of public office or possessed of private means. He, on the other hand, was a working hack, absolutely dependent on the output of his pen. Easy to commune with nature – or the Oversoul – if you have the leisure. Not so easy, when creditors are at the door. Poe may have been snobbishly suspicious of "the mob", but he claimed a certain kinship and empathy with his readers and, again in contrast to the social and spiritual remoteness of the New England writers, was prepared to offer his readers a glimpse behind the scenes, however partial, rationalising or plain fictitious it might be.

Poe's belief, as expressed in "The Philosophy of Composition", that works of literary art had a "distinct limit", that of a single sitting, are a function of that haste. He believed that poetry was effective when short, rather than epical or musing, and that short stories were more creatively challenging than novels. Not everything Poe said was simple rationalisation; his preference for short fiction was undoubtedly coloured by the imbroglio of *Pym*, but *Pym* was also typical of a man working beyond his natural reach and span. Poe had no strong affection for the mass, but he gauged its appetite very precisely, and as a kind of modernist recognised that the urban reader of the future would be conditioned by the accelerating haste of modern life. Hence, again, short tales and poems devised to deliver a single, devastating effect.

Poe said that his raven was intended to convey remembrance *"Mournful and Never-Ending"*. Its familiar music, with the long vowel sounds of "Lenore" and *"Nevermore"*, was and is easily parodied and is perhaps too laboured. Poe had not been publishing – which is not to say that he had not been writing – much poetry since he moved to New York. The only new poem of 1844 was "Dreamland", which includes the couplet "Mountains toppling evermore / Into seas without a shore": sign, perhaps, that his imagination was running on the same mournful chord through the period. The critical debates in which he was again to be enmeshed ran much on questions of plagiarism, always a favourite weapon of literary flyting. Poe would later accuse Henry Wadsworth Longfellow of literary theft. Just a few weeks before "The Raven" was first published, Poe had a squib in the *Southern Literary Messenger* called "The Literary Life of Thingum Bob", in which magazine editors – Poe made the mistake of naming at least one powerful name – are unable to recognize work sent to them as original that is actually made up of tags and quotes from the classics.

Poe was himself borrowing and self-plagiarising in "The Raven". Its cadences are almost over-familiar from his earlier verse, and it's interesting that "The Philosophy of Composition", unlike the later, better and arguably more sincere "The Rationale of Verse" has nothing of interest to say about prosody. T. S. Eliot may have been right when he said that if Poe were serious about his ideas of composition he might have taken greater care with his poem, which has a thudding obviousness. It did, however, catch the ear of Robert Browning. His wife Elizabeth Barrett may well have been mollified by having the 1845 volume *The Raven and other poems* dedicated to her as "The Noblest of her Sex" and while she was grateful for Poe's review of her work in the *Broadway Journal*, she was also slightly embarrassed by it, and, rather than indulge in too much mutual appreciation, she attributed her admiration to both Robert and her father; she may, in addition, have recognised that some of Poe's music – including a strategic use of "evermore" – owed something to her own "Lady Geraldine's Courtship". Other sources are more obvious. Poe had shown an interest in *Barnaby Rudge*, an obvious source for his bird of ill-omen, though his need for a "non-reasoning creature, capable of speech" sounds like a neat inversion of the murderous, quasi-vocal ape in "The Murders on the Rue Morgue". Later, when he was mired in "The Little Longfellow war", an ally of the older poet suggested that Poe had also drawn on popular verses called "The Bird of the Dream". To dwell on the poem's scattered elements, though, is to cede some credibility to the mechanistic production process described in "The Philosophy of Composition".

Elizabeth Barrett's praise was important to Poe, who wanted and to some extent won both popular and critical success with his raven. The circumstances of the poem's writing have been much discussed and mythologised; the circumstances of its actual publication ought to be clearer, but even here there are some typical confusions and complications. Though "The Raven" first appeared in the *Evening Mirror* – the daily newspaper which had partly replaced the revived (by Willis and George Pope Morris) *Weekly Mirror* – he had previously sold the poem to the Whig *American Review*, edited by George H. Colton as a journal of politics, literature and – an ongoing obsession of Poe's – science. He would subsequently reprint it elsewhere, including in the *Broadway Journal* – by then, his own. The poem's appearance in the *Mirror* in advance of the *Review*, where it was credited to "—Quarles", was apparently by arrangement, but Willis and Morris had a certain leverage, in that Poe had been working for them as critic and sub-editor since October 1844; in the circumstances, it would have been hard to deny them the coup.

As ever, Poe was desperate for funds. Though the flow of great stories had been staunched by daily journey-work, he continued to write at an extraordinary rate. Shortly after signing up with the *Mirror*, he began publication, in the *Democratic Review*, of the "Marginalia" that would occupy him almost to his death. Essentially these were short essays on divers topics – often lifted, though with much editorial care and attention to style, from Poe's omnivorous reading.

Two other important things happened in January 1845. First, Poe renewed contact with his future nemesis Rufus Griswold, who was editing a prose anthology and a new edition of the *Poets and Poetry of America*. As Quinn's meticulous research has shown, Griswold subsequently doctored the correspondence by inventing long passages in which Poe seems to flatter him in the most abject way, expressing gratitude for favours that never existed other than in

Griswold's imagination, hinting that Griswold's imprimatur would benefit Poe's future prospects, and inserting fictitious asides like "I say this not because you praised me: everybody praises me now ... " which make Poe sound like a complacent egomaniac.

Fortunately, Poe had more honest and straightforward friends than this. The other important event of January 1845 was the establishment by Charles F. Briggs and John Brisco of the *Broadway Journal*. Thanks to the recommendation of James Russell Lowell (a pen-friend, really; they met just once that summer, though Lowell befriended Mrs Clemm after Edgar's death), Poe was taken on as assistant editor in February, clearly on a cautious, probationary basis – he now came trailing a certain reputation for erratic behaviour – but as a business partner. A rider to his contract severed the arrangement should he default. In addition, Briggs and Brisco stated clearly in their welcome notice of Poe's and music editor Henry C. Watson's arrival that the paper would avoid "personalities"; in other words, *ad hominem* criticism would not be tolerated.

Poe may have mostly kept sober and attended to his duties – he certainly produced a substantial quantity of copy – but he either overlooked or was not minded to follow this last stricture. He had already taken up rather personal cudgels in the *Evening* (and *Weekly*) *Mirror,* suggesting that in a commercial anthology called *The Waif*, personally selected by Henry Wadsworth Longfellow, the older poet had purposely avoided surrounding himself with any American poets who might challenge his pre-eminence, preferring the company of Robert Browning and Percy Bysshe Shelley; this despite Poe's strong admiration for Longfellow's work. He then compounded the insult by suggesting that one of the poems selected was plagiarised from Thomas Hood, an easily dis-proved anachronism.

The debate raged across both *Mirror* and *Broadway Journal,* and flared elsewhere when Poe suggested that Longfellow's reputation was largely due to his academic chair at Harvard and to having married a wealthy woman. Poe's fellow-editors and publishers tried to calm matters down, while Poe himself grew ever shriller as rebuttals and counter-accusations made their way into print. "The Raven" had also appeared in the *Journal* – as many of Poe's poems and stories would now that he had a ready outlet – and Poe's recent celebrity disinclined him to hear anything that ques-tioned its originality or merit. Controversy had the same effect on Poe as wine; he was no more temperate in his opin-ions than he was with alcohol when the fit was on him; but he must have been possessed by what he himself once called "The Imp of the Perverse" when he decided to accuse, not just the minor James Aldrich, but also the admired Longfel-low of plagiarism. Poe suggested that Longfellow had passed off translation as original creation, but more extraordinary still suggested that other work of Longfellow's bore a striking resemblance to his own disastrous "Politian".

As so often with Poe, it is hard to know what to make of this. Plagiarism is a relatively serious charge, though to be fair the headline "Longfellow and other plagiarists" under which the relevant columns were subsequently collected in *Literati of New York City* was not Poe's but – and it's prob-ably no longer surprising to read this – Rufus Griswold's. Even so, why suggest that a respected artist has stolen from a failed work rather than a masterpiece? Not, surely, because there is less chance of detection? The motivation is complex, but might it not be that in the fever which always seemed to grip Poe when he entered the lists of literary feuding there surfaced an opportunity to remind a neglectful public of a neglected work, still sentimentally cherished by its author? It isn't unusual for authors of long-forgotten works to claim that they have been pilfered, in the hope that the scandal might lead to their being reprinted or simply read again. Maybe Poe still had hopes of his poetic drama. Or could it be that he regarded literary flyting as a game with few rules and no restraints, where the details of an accusation were less important than the wit which accompanied it?

To his credit, Longfellow did not respond directly, though he had enough allies – Poe, typically, continued to insist that he was one of them – to ensure that the charge did not go unchallenged. The most serious casualty of the "Longfellow war" was Poe's friendship with James Russell Lowell. Like most of his more understanding supporters, Lowell was aware that Poe's aberrations, including his drinking, were to some degree involuntary. However, Lowell was dismayed by the tenor of the Longfellow controversy, and his attitude may have hardened when Poe surrendered to his imp again and this time accused Lowell of stealing – from Wordsworth, which might be deemed more flattering – but stealing nonetheless.

Lowell had clearly had enough, but nursed his wrath more privily, and only in 1848 published the lines in "A Fable for Critics" that won him a small, witty revenge: "Here comes Poe with his Raven like Barnaby Rudge, / Three fifths of him genius and two fifths sheer fudge". Poe didn't like it, but it was a hard verdict to gainsay at the time and in the circumstances. Lowell still worked on Poe's behalf and even organised a public reading for him in Boston, where he delivered "Al Aaraaf" and "The Raven", but failed to proffer a new work of the didactic or philosophical sort a New England audience seemed to expect. Poe did not write occasional pieces, and a proportion of the audience reportedly walked. Poe seems to have had a drink at some stage of the visit and, as a result, delivered himself of a very negative opinion of his birth-place, its literary manners and some of its most distinguished inhabitants. The scandal rumbled up and down from North to South for some weeks, but by then Poe was emboldened by a freshly found editorial authority.

If Poe still harped to friends and family about having his own magazine, he was moving closer to it by an unexpected and not entirely desirable route. As ever, it isn't clear what lay behind the rift, but by mid-summer of 1845, Briggs was no longer involved in the *Broadway Journal* and Poe had a contract which guaranteed him freedom from interference in editorial matters; he also had a 50/50 share with Brisco in whatever profits there might be. More important, Poe's editorial role reintroduced Poe to the world of American theatre, about which he wrote in his magazine, though with less passion than he brought to scientific subjects and the hobby-horse of plagiarism; more importantly, and coupled with the success of "The Raven", it provided him with an entré into the literary salons of New York which provided him with the kind of company – wealthy, intelligent older women in the main – that would sustain him and spark the curious, part-sexual, part-sentimental flirtations that would punctuate his last years, a very American variant on the conventions of courtly troubadour love.

A week after the Boston imbroglio, and with the papers buzzing with charge and countercharge about it, Poe paid Brisco $50 with a note for further settlement, and took sole possession of the journal. He beggared himself in the process and was at once writing letters to old friends, associates and even family – John Pendleton Kennedy, Griswold, George Poe – asking for loans. Winning the *Journal* was a pyrrhic victory for he found himself master of a financial ruin and one as far as can be conceived from the well-printed and intelligent monthly he had dreamed of with the chimerical *The Penn* and *Stylus*. As early as December, he was obliged to sell half his interest in the *Broadway Journal* to a Thomas Lane. All he really kept from the deal was the drudgery of editing the magazine, which sometimes occupied sixteen hours a day; by his own account, but believable given the amount of work, new and revised, that he put into it. He was writing so much he had to adopt a pseudonym, "Littleton Barry", for some pieces.

A year that began in high promise ended in disappointment. Poe had stirred New York with his bird of ill omen, he had rattled the latches and letter-boxes of Boston; he had (briefly) had his magazine and his coterie of admiring poetesses; he had seen a collection of his *Tales* published in book form and had managed to save some of his poems from further revision and mis-printing by seeing them bound together as *The Raven and Other Poems* (the stories had sold well enough to merit the latter's publication in November; Poe had very little hand in the selection of material in either case). He had also managed to write some interesting stories and see them published by magazines that must by then have seemed reliable, long-term beacons in a working life that consisted mostly of shoals.

"The Imp of the Perverse" appeared in *Graham's* in July. The thin murder plot is little more than a retread of "The Black Cat", which he had published in the *Saturday Evening Post* in August 1843 and it somewhat resembles "The Tell-Tale Heart", too, but "The Imp of the Perverse" (an expression

Poe may have coined or read elsewhere) is as much essay as story, an analysis of the self-destructive urge that leads us to perform the very actions we know we should not. It is also a strong articulation of Poe's resistance to the optimistic, progressivist philosophy of those complacent New England Transcendentalists with whom he clashed. The "Bostonian" conviction that the grandest designs of God can be read in the smallest details of nature. "The intellectual or logical man, rather than the understanding or observant man, set himself to imagine designs – to dictate purposes to God. Having thus fathomed, to his satisfaction, the intentions of Jehovah, out of these intentions he built his innumerable systems of mind.... If we cannot comprehend God in his visible works, how then in his inconceivable thoughts, that call the world into being?" This is as much about creativity as it is about metaphysics, for Poe regards the imagination itself, in league with a mind as scientifically fascinated as his own, as dealing largely with horrors. "We stand upon the brink of a precipice. We peer into the abyss – we grow sick and dizzy. Our first impulse is to shrink away from the danger. Unaccountably we remain ... it is but a thought, although a fearful one, and one which chills the very marry of our bones with the fierceness of the delight of its horror. It is merely the idea of what would be our sensations during the sweeping precipitancy of a fall from such a height ... for this very cause do we now the most vividly desire it." This is written a decade before the birth of Sigmund Freud – who always credited "the poets" with the discovery of the unconscious – and some fifty years before he offered the first topology of the psyche and operations like repression, in *The Interpretation of Dreams* (1899). Does it not also conjure up a Poe who gazes at the brandy bottle, knowing that it contains an abyss but desiring it fiercely? Or who looked at Virginia, and saw only death? Or who could look from a his manuscripts on one side of the desk and a pile of unpaid bills on the other, and craved nothing more than his own destruction?

There is certainly a morbidity in Poe's writing at this time. Five years before, in "The Man of the Crowd", he had been able to consider obsessive loneliness with a degree of detachment, via a logical narrator. Now, though, even in a story of ratiocination, the scientific persona barely seems in control. In December 1845, *American Review* ran what was originally called "The Facts of M. Valdemar's Case" (known later as "The Facts in the Case of M. Valdemar"), an extraordinarily squeamish story in which a dying man is hypnotised and kept "alive" for many months, only to deliquesce obscenely as soon as the trance is lifted. As so often with Poe, the line between fact and fancy was blurred and the story was reprinted as a pamphlet in Britain the following year. For threepence, a curious public could read the thoughts of "Edgar Allan Poe esq of New York" on *Mesmerism, "In Articulo Mortis". An Astounding and Horrifying Narrative. Shewing the Extraordinary Power of Mesmerism in arresting the Progress of Death"*.

If depression is a kind of trance, it had Poe in its grip from this point on. His waking dreams remained familiar enough: to own a literary magazine of serious intent, not a rag like the *Broadway Journal*; to live in domestic bliss with Virginia; to enjoy the attention of literary ladies, like Mrs Frances Sargent Osgood, whose friendship with Poe was cannily encouraged by Virginia since there seemed less risk of sexual entanglement in it than in some of his flirtations with the kind of New York ladies who collected poets and other romantic rascals. But they were dreams that seemed less and less contiguous with reality. Poe's life was drifting into the kinds of nightmare that had long crowded his fiction.

10

"To the few who love me and whom I love": Poe's later work, 1846–8

The *Broadway Journal* limped into a new year, but on January 3 1846, Poe announced that "unexpected engagements" demanded his full attention and that he was closing the magazine, with a cordial farewell to his foes as well as his friends. Poe was inclined privately to pass off the magazine's demise as, if anything, a good thing, since it left his way clear to establish the long dream of literary monthly, but that was mere bravado and rationalisation. In some respects, the *Journal*'s early demise is puzzling. Poe had some reputation for building circulation and his ability to play off friends and foes in print was good magazining. If all that was required was steady effort, then Poe seems the ideal man for the job; if what was needed was investment, then clearly he wasn't.

It is pointless to speculate, but if the *Broadway Journal* had continued publication through the spring and summer of 1846, it might well have survived, even in a treacherous market. The truth was that Poe was in the grip of a serious melancholia and physical debility; modern medicine might diagnose clinical depression and chronic fatigue. The almost demonic energy he had shown at *Graham's* was gone. To take a measure of the change in him, certainly as it might be thought to impact on his literary style, one might look at "The Cask of Amontillado", written early in 1846 but only published in the late autumn in *Godey's Lady's Book*, where he was also still able to publish signed notices and reviews.

It is again a murder fantasy, one of the best of the later arabesques, but it is written in a markedly terse, almost clipped style, in sentences that seldom exceed a dozen words, the dialogue mostly in elided phrases. The narrator Montresor tells how, in revenge for unspecified hurts and insults, he lures another nobleman Fortunato into his cellars on the pretext of sampling a pipe of amontillado which he has procured at a suspiciously low price. Fortunato, a noted connoisseur, is already drunk, however, and wearing carnival motley. When they arrive at a distant niche, deep underground, Montresor shackles his enemy to the wall and begins the process of bricking him up. In tones of utmost neutrality, he listens to the doomed man cry and whimper as the realisation of a horrific fate rapidly sobers him. The story ends as abruptly as it began with the revelation that the events in question happened half a century before and that the crime remains undetected and unsolved. The final words are "*Requiescat in pace*", spoken by the murderer to the memory of his victim.

There is much to unpack here. The story has various literary antecedents, which is typical of Poe's widely scattered reading and the synthetic retentiveness of his memory. Its purely formal characteristics are difficult to disentangle from what it suggests about Poe's putative mental state at the time. There is no female presence in the story for a change, and certainly no return from the other side; the clanking of the chains ceases with Fortunato's last breath. It is significant

that alcohol is the crux of the story and that it should be associated with involuntary loss of freedom and ultimately death.

It may be, though, that psychological extrapolation is the
wrong way to approach "The Cask of Amontillado". One
hesitates to conclude that the story's staccato measures are
a sign of Poe's exhaustion – he soon resumed a more florid
style in the vast prose poem *Eureka* – or that the apparent
lack of detail suggest scantness of imagination. In fact, the
story has considerable detail and much of it potentially very
telling. Fortunato has a bad cough but boldly says he won't
die of it; in the end, of course, he doesn't, but someone close
to Poe was about to. As the two men pass through the vaults,
Montresor describes his family's coat of arms, which shows
a golden foot stamping on a snake that his bitten the heel,
and following a strange Masonic gesture of Fortunato's he
pretends to be of the craft himself, though the trowel he pro-
duces from his cloak is, of course, an instrument of murder
rather than of ritual.

Given Poe's self-destructive battles with fellow-critics and
editors – perhaps that is what is behind those insults and inju-
ries left curiously unspecified at the start of the story – might
not that strange emblem be a representation of his literary
predicament, with himself as the turning worm with still-
dangerous fangs? The Montresor family motto is given as
Nemo me impune lacessit (who dares meddle with me?) which
Poe might well have seen in Scotland. Did he believe that there
were Masons among his tormentors, or did he simply blame a
less specific freemasonry of establishment writers? Which did
he desire more: revenge or peace? The story's final blessing
quivers with ironies. Here is a writer who had never previously allowed any victim – deserving or otherwise – to rest
in unambiguous peace. Perhaps, he now craved nothing less

than that for himself. He may also have recognised that, like Fortunato, he had been the architect of his own downfall. Having insulted others in print so many times, he could only now watch those insults come home to roost. In February 1847, he would win $225 in damages from a libel suit, but like the victory of that golden foot, it was to be a pyrrhic one; Poe got his money, but at the same time surrendered much of his remaining reputation and said an anguished farewell to loyal helpmeet and supporter. If at the beginning of 1846, he lost his magazine, at the beginning of the following year, he lost his beloved Virginia.

All this is psychological extrapolation. From another viewpoint, "The Cask of Amontillado" is a more technical exercise in carefully elided and unembellished narrative and an attempt to catch something of the cold amorality of the psychopath. We hear in Montresor's neutral narrative striking anticipations of modern serial killers like Hannibal Lecter. Needless to say, even a technical exercise can reveal much about its writer, but it is probably better to emphasise the story's mastery rather than its author's presumed state of mind.

Either way, Virginia's cough and other outward signs of worsening health would by this time have been painfully evident and unavoidable in the tiny cottage they now occupied some dozen miles north of New York, at Fordham, in what is now the Bronx. Poe did his best to portray it as a domestic idyll, except to friends like Thomas Holley Chivers, who he had once described as "one of the best and one of the worst poets in America. His productions affect one as a wild dream – strange incongruous, full of images of more than arabesque monstrosity": Poe might have been writing about himself! To Chivers, he confesses that he has been "dreadfully ill" and in "dreadful poverty", assailed by "the flocks of little birds of prey that always take the opportunity of illness to peck at a sick fowl of larger dimensions". He explains to Chivers that letters have taken months to reach him since he, Virginia and Mrs Clemm had to abandon the boarding house at 195 East Broadway on poor terms with the landlady.

Poe had described Chivers in his "Autography", but now he was at it again, publishing in the May 1846 edition of *Godey's* the first instalment of a series called "The Literati of New York City. Some Honest Opinions at Random Respecting their Authorial Merits, with Occasional Words of Personality". With extraordinary disengenuousness, Poe later explained to a young admirer that the series had been suspended because some of his subjects understood his words to be critical rather than merely "critical gossip". It seems too fine a line, particularly given those "Occasional Words of Personality". Most of the pieces concern writers who have all but disappeared from the literary record and are valuable for that, but the tone of his attacks on others was bound to attract the attention of those small birds of prey, particularly when he followed up with plangent statements of his own physical state: "Am now scarcely able to write even this letter". One Thomas Dunn English responded in kind – the old familiar charges of plagiarism and forgery – and in terms that even Rufus Griswold thought unnecessarily harsh. Poe sued and eventually won, but before he received his damages his world fell apart.

On January 30 1847, Virginia Clemm Poe died at home. She was buried nearby and later reinterred with her husband in Baltimore. The story that she gave a deathbed blessing to Poe's romance with one Mary Devereaux – "Poe's Mary" – is a much later confection from a magazine story published in the late 1880s, when a woman tried to capitalise on the poet's pop-star reputation by claiming a long-term affair. In truth, Poe did have many women looking out for him. Even in her grief, Mrs Clemm seems to have been all practicality and support, and a Mrs Shew, who had some medical understanding, was a genuine and practical help both to the dying Virginia and her prostrated husband. In a poem published in March, Poe thanked her "For the resurrection of deep buried faith / In Truth, in Virtue, in Humanity".

One naturally searches for poetic responses to the death of Virginia, too, and it is easy enough to find them in the most significant poem he published in 1847. The very name and title "Ulalume" suggests ululation and grief, and is sufficiently close to other "L" names – Ligeia, Eulalie, Annabel Lee – to fit with Poe's *idée fixe* about the death of a beautiful woman as a poetic subject. On the other hand, it is known that "Ulalume" was written – begun, at least – as an elocution piece for the Rev. Cotesworth Bronson, who gave lectures on the art of public speaking. It is again a poem that aims to deliver a calculated musical effect – Aldous Huxley called it a "carapace of jewelled sound" – rather than a clear narrative or emotional impact. But unlike "The Raven", which builds steadily to a pre-determined climax, "Ulalume" disintegrates into virtual meaninglessness in its final measures, some indication that Poe may as he finished it have been working under severe psychological pressure rather than exerting artistic command. When Rufus Griswold republished the verses, he excluded the final stanza, which seems to have accorded with Poe's own wishes.

In sere October weather and at nightfall, the speaker of the poem walks along lost in dialogue with his own soul, unconscious of his direction until he realises that he has come to the grave of his lost Ulalume, who died on the same day a year before. There are oddities about the description of Ulalume in the poem; she/it is referred to as a "secret" and as a "thing" in that chaotic final stanza, though the latter may mean her monument. The drama of the piece is between the lure of Astarté and that of the Moon. Poe was well enough versed in ancient mythologies to know the significance of Astarté/Ishtar/Venus as an expression of sexual desire and fertility. Among the *Tamerlane* poems was the later rejected "Evening Star", which contrasted Venus and the Moon in similar terms to those of "Astarté" and "Dian" in "Ulalume".

If the poem can be unpacked psychologically it seems to suggest that in Virginia Poe had a life-partner who addressed both his physical and his spiritual needs – an interpretation that settles any squeamish uncertainty about the nature of their marriage, just as eyewitness accounts of the Poe home settle any question about Virginia's natural refinement and intelligence – but who has now been taken from him. The speaker recognises that Astarté is "warmer" than Dian: "rolls", "revels", "sighs" have an unmistakable sexual tinge to which the poet's troubled psyche warns him; it is also she who reminds him that the monument they happen across is Ulalume's. The picture is of a man benighted and in grief, prey to sexual longings and other appetites – an awkward courtship of Sarah Helen Whitman in his final two years was an often embarrassing mixture of callow passion, intellectual high-mindedness and actual intoxication – who can only be steadied by keeping the iconic memory of Virginia whole and before him.

Virginia's death did seem to cut Poe adrift, and leave him prey to unwise passions and to the lionizing instincts of New York ladies, in which sympathy, condescension and the frisson of "dangerous" company weighed equally. Poe was drinking again, if he had ever really stopped, and again adducing poverty and either anxiety or grief over Virginia's plight as the reason. He had been incensed when just after Christmas 1846, Nathaniel Willis had published an editorial in the *Home Journal* revealing his former associate's alcoholism and lamenting the inability to help "*disabled labourers with the brain*". Poe's correspondence of the period alternates between abject confessions of the impact of even a single glass of wine and bright assurances that he has not touched a drop for many weeks, a familiar enough self-contradiction among alcoholics. That angered him most, though, was Willis's suggestion that he and Virginia were without friends. How good those friends were, and how true, is harder to determine.

How good "Ulalume" is is equally difficult. It certainly lacks the organic form and unified music of "The Raven", and it has little of the simple beauty of Poe's last completed poem "Annabel Lee", which again returned to the theme of death and beauty. The lapse of its final stanza is unprecedented, but much of the rest of it is not quite up to standard. When Thomas Holley Chivers spitefully suggested that Poe had plagiarised it from him, he somehow confirmed his own banality: imitation of a poetaster like Chivers could only yield indifferent results. If "The Philosophy of Composition" was a companion piece to "The Raven", then "Ulalume" was also awkwardly shadowed by an essay called "The Rationale of Verse". The latter had been accepted by George Colton for the *American Review* but he had not published the piece and in the event exchanged it for Poe's poem; the essay eventually appeared in the *Southern Literary Messenger* in the autumn of 1848. There is little question of playfulness or rationalisation after the fact here. Poe was lecturing on a subject of which he knew less than he intuited. His extraordinary ear was not matched by a sound understanding of the history of English prosody and it is "Ulalume" rather than "The Raven" that reads as if it has been written according to a poorly learned formula. The very self-consciousness Poe had used as a device in his literary games worked against him here.

"Ulalume" is also a poem whose language lurches awkwardly between the conventionally "poetic" and the scientific: "scoriac", "boreal", "nebulous", "liquescent". If his caprice for Bronson was lent unintended resonance by the death of Virginia, Poe was at the same time embarked on a work that took both his understanding of poetic language and of science into a new real, but also confirmed that Poe worked best and most truly when he relied on his intuitions and his ear.

ooooo

His last great work was certainly written at the dictate of ear and intuition; indeed, *Eureka* celebrates them. Modern criticism accepts that it *is* a great work and more recent interpretations have tended to accept Poe's own insistence that *Eureka* is a "prose poem" rather than the scientific treatise it almost ironically purports to be, or the ravings of a damaged mind.

As with much of Poe's discursive writing, it is necessary to deal with the "almost-irony" first of all. He was addicted to the hoax, to tongue-in-cheek burlesque and to a tone of knowing complicity which allows him to address his intellectual peers as well as talk down to the bulk of his audience. To be fair, the tone of *Eureka* is largely determined by its origins in a public lecture Poe was invited to give at the Society Library; it is another work for speaking, and for performance, and its manner comes in part from that. Poe had known his parents for too little time to have a natural gift for the stage. As ever, though, he needed money, and had not entirely abandoned the notion of founding his magazine. His self-deprecation is both a rhetorical device and a way of expressing a kind of nervous contempt for an occasion which, after the Boston imbroglio, must have made him anxious even as it fuelled his self-loathing at having to address the herd for dollars. In a bid to be disarming, he even offers a hostage to critical fortune by suggesting that many of his listeners will consider him a "madman" when they hear what he has to say.

In the event, most of those who turned out to hear him – it was apparently an atrocious night – merely found "On The Cosmography of the Universe", as it was originally entitled, confusing, boring and, at two hours, overlong; in its finished version, *Eureka* is as long as this small book. It is not true to say that the piece was universally derided at the time of its publication but most of the positive comment was directed to the original lecture. Later readers, who had time to dwell on Poe's logic, found it preposterous or, in the case of Mrs Shew, blasphemous.

Poe appeared to the Society Library audience almost as the wandering thinker in "Ulalume". He gave his address just days after the first anniversary of Virginia's death and funeral. Like most of his important works, it had probably been in draft for some time, and certainly even before the invitation to speak. At one level, *Eureka* is a meditation on death and an attempt to provide not so much a religious or spiritual consolation as a cosmological one. For an artist so obsessed with the integrity of the individual and the survival of the self, to contemplate the universe was to be both overwhelmed and reassured.

Great claims have often been made for the scientific content of *Eureka*: that in its discussion of *"the Original Unity of the First Thing"* it anticipates the Big Bang theory of the universe's origin, and even more startlingly, the Big Crunch that will return it to a single primal particle; that he makes reference to something like black holes, which would not even be theoretically postulated for another century; that he imagined a non-Euclidean universe; that he understands matter to be nothing more than attraction and repulsion; that he proposed a convincing solution to "Olbers' paradox", which asks why if the universe is infinite, thus implying a radiant star in every line of sight, the night sky is not luminous instead of dark. To be sure, Poe's response to the latter question, which drew on ideas of Johannes Kepler and others, but had only been published in its iconic form in 1826, has been accepted as partially correct: "The only mode, therefore, in which, under such a state of affairs, we could comprehend the voids which our telescopes find in innumerable directions, would be by supposing the distance of the invisible background so immense that no ray from it has yet been able to reach us at all." However, all this shows is that Poe was of sufficiently sharp intelligence to think through the problem. Neither here, nor in any of his other apparent anticipations of 20th century cosmological science, is he doing anything more than indulging in speculation, and in the kind of ratiocination he had attributed in fiction to Dupin. This is, indeed, a form of science fiction, a genre which does on occasion throw up startling "predictions" of future discoveries.

By far the weakest chapter in Arthur Hobson Quinn's iconic biography is the one devoted to *Eureka*, largely because Quinn seems concerned with nothing more than testing Poe's ideas against contemporary scientific understanding; Quinn was writing in 1941, when the two theories of relativity, the nature of the quantum and the possibility of exploring the subatomic realm were all new enough to make it seem that Poe was more prescient than was in fact the case. Less frequently commented on is Poe's apparent anticipation of the Jungian collective unconscious when he refers to not just a physical but also metaphysical and spitual Big Crunch when the "final ingathering" of humankind takes place. Many objected to the pantheistic tone of the lecture and essay, but it aligned Poe with unexpected closeness to the Transcendentalist philosophies he had so vigorously opposed in his attacks on "Frogpondium"; to what extent these differences were philosophical and to what extent literary and political is now hard to disentangle. Ultimately, though, what is more important about *Eureka* than its chance consonance with later research is its tone and form. Recent critics have revalued the work largely because its philosophical premises – fundamentally that of the closed universe obedient to single laws, but also the notion that the universe is God's text and "plot" – are strikingly consistent with Poe's literary aesthetics.

He himself asked that the work be judged according to those principles. A strangely touching dedication addresses the work "To the few who love me and whom I love – to those who feel rather than to those who think – to the dreamers and those who put faith in dreams as in the only realities – I offer this Book of Truths, not in its character of Truth-Teller, but for the Beauty that abounds in its Truth … " He subsequently declares that he wishes the work to be read only as a poem when he is gone. Truth and beauty are routinely juggled and combined in poetic manifestos, but Poe takes the matter further. If he seems prescient regarding modern science, he also anticipates much of modern linguistic theory and structuralism. For Poe, language – and particularly written language – has an absolute primacy. Just as the universe is conjured up out of nothing by God, so the writer conjures up a rich peopled reality out of white paper and black ink. Poe's resistance to logic and rationality led him to consider extremes of sensation and the very foundations of the self, but it also persuaded him that the highly specific consonances and dissonances, rhymes and metres of poetic language there was a profound generative process at work.

In *Eureka,* he depended somewhat on his reading in the scientific literature of the time, much of which would nowadays be considered para-science, but he was ultimately more concerned with the sheer cumulative power of words to create meaning, independent of and, for Poe, superior to empirical research. In this and much else, he greatly resembles a later but equally scandalous American writer, Norman Mailer. Like Poe and at about the same age, Mailer had delighted in delivering barbed assessements of his contemporaries, many of them friends. His "Quick and Expensive Comments on the Talent in the Room", originally in the *Village Voice* – which he helped to found – and later in the collection *Advertisements for Myself*, is a direct descendant of Poe's "Autography" and "Literati of New York City". More important, though, is Mailer's almost obsessive interest in what can only be described as existentialist religion, a complex dialectic of God and the Devil, sex, cowardice, alcohol, plastic, cancer, time and death, usually interwoven into narratives which, again like Poe's, seem neither "fiction" nor "non-fiction" in the usual sense. Mailer's life-long obsession with the novel, a term he frequently applied to works of reportage, is similar to Poe's insistence that *Eureka* is a form of poetry. Even more fundamentally, though, the two writers tended to bombard a subject, even one in which they could claim no real expertise, to the point where the sheer saturation of language generates an impression of profound significance. Often in Mailer, one is convinced by the cadence rather than the logic or the evidence, and much the same was true of Poe. Recent philosophers of a science, from Sir Arthur Eddington to Gary Zukav and Stephen Hawking, have alluded to an unexpected closeness between mysticism and the scientific method, whereby intuition and research yield strikingly similar conclusions. It is less surprising, nonetheless, that Poe should have stumbled across so many approximations of later discoveries than that he should have written in such an openly mystical way at all. Much in *Eureka* resembles the despised approach and style of "Frogpondium".

The same rhetoric method was raised to the highest degree by the greatest of all the rising New England novelists, Herman Melville. In *Moby-Dick,* a vast accretion of cetological facts leads inexorably to the revelation of the White Whale. The style and manner of Melville's early South Seas books is very different to Poe's, but there are obvious connections between them and *Pym*, and between the enigmatic ending of *Pym* and *Moby-Dick*. The two men did not meet, but Poe had some contact with Melville's supporter and friend Nathaniel Hawthorne, whose *Twice Told Tales* and *Mosses from an Old Manse* he had reviewed – and in the process discussed his own theories of the short tale – in the November 1847 issue of *Godey's Lady's Book*. Poe had for some time been aware of his quiet rival up in Salem. The previous year Hawthorne had written to thank him for earlier notices whose robust tone he preferred to "a sugared falsehood. I confess, however, that I admire you rather as a writer of tales than as a critic upon them."

Around the same time, Poe's work was beginning to appear – albeit very freely translated or adapted – in France, where his reputation would soon be greater than at home. "The Gold Bug" appeared in *Revue Britannique* in 1845, as "Le Scarabée d'or". Three years later, Charles Baudelaire produced his version of "Mesmeric Revelation", the moment which began Poe's reign as presiding deity of the Symbolist movement. Poe was not entirely neglected at home, but much of the attention he received was either hostile or fawning. He had attracted a circle of ladies, often with the resources to pay him to assess or to edit their own verses, and with whom he began a series of embarrassing flirtations and romances. He could not quite keep his eyes on Ulalume's tomb.

At least one of these ladies, and probably the brightest of them, was disinclined to continue the friendship long after Virginia's death. Mrs Shew was disturbed by *Eureka*, but was almost certainly also concerned by Poe's bouts of drinking and the importunate behavious that accompanied them. Some found a certain nobility in his prose poem, most found it abstruse and confusing, and an easy work to attribute to drink, or madness. Modern critics may value *Eureka*. Poe certainly overvalued it, allegedly suggesting that it was a more important work than Newton's discovery of gravity and insisting that a million copies – some versions say 50,000 – be printed. His publisher did not value it quite so highly. George P. Putnam, late of Wiley & Putnam and the man who had brought out *Pym* in England, ran off some 750 copies and sold 500 at 75 cents. He gave Poe $14 as an advance. Ever willing to tempt fate, Poe told Mrs Clemm that he could now die content, knowing his great project was complete. *Eureka* was just another work that would not see a second edition in its author's lifetime.

11

"I must die": Poe's final year, 1848–49

A daguerreotype taken in Providence, Rhode Island, catches Edgar Allan Poe in the last full year of his life. If it were the only such image of him, it would have an interesting effect on our image of the man. What is immediately interesting is how well it squares with the most positive descriptions of him, and how badly with the received notion of a *poète maudit* of disordered personality, given over to alcohol. The clothes, coat, waistcoat, white shirt and cravat, are shabby but the effect is dapper, and the popped buttons of the vest – easy to imagine the poet absent-mindedly tucking a hand inside as he discoursed – are the only untidy aspect. The hair is thinnish and straggly and the dark moustache turns down slightly on the left hand side, not so much contemptuous as suggesting a potential for contempt. The forehead is huge and pale, but it is the eyes – even given the fixity of expression that came with the long poses required of early photographic sitters – that arrest the attention: liquid, dark, melancholy and penetrating. It is not, on the surface at least, the image of a man who last lost his grip on reality.

There is, however, another image from around the same time. This time the portrait is taken full face and against a broodingly dark background and framed by fuller, seemingly blacker hair. Poe is similarly dressed, respectable enough, but hardly stylish. The hand is indeed stuffed inside his waistcoat. The difference is in his face, which is reversed in one or other of these images, because the mouth droops on the opposite side. The high forehead is so white as to give off light, the eyes are pouched and deeply hooded at looking at a point high over the daguerrotypist's shoulder. The gaze is full of a kind of baleful sorrow. It is not that of a man at ease with himself or at ease with the world. He looks like a bird of ill omen.

In 1848, Poe was not mad, but he was certainly susceptible. He fell in love on the instant. He still believed he would have his magazine. He had some notion that all the wrongs of his childhood and youth could be put right. That is partly why he went back to Richmond in the summer of 1849. A fresh opportunity to run a magazine had presented itself, and after a dozen bruising years in New York, Poe was minded to return "home", where there was still unfinished emotional business. He planned to and probably made a short visit to the city the summer before, but the evidence is contradictory. None of the Virginia papers made any reference to his presence, and it seems unlikely that someone of his celebrity would have been overlooked. Then, the stories that posthumously circulated about the visit were garish in the extreme: that Poe had fought a duel, that he had tried to revive his teenage relationship with Sarah Elmira Royster, now Mrs Shelton; and that, either in disappointment at rejection or because he was now so far gone in morals as to be beyond restraint, he had spent three weeks in an extended debauch in the city's dockside stews.

Most of this can be dismissed fairly readily, though it

remains possible that he was there, and somewhat probable that if he did make the proposed visit, there was a romantic as well as a professional motive. The story of Poe's day to day activities between Virginia's death and his own makes for uneasy reading. It is often only possible to locate him precisely by reference to one or other of the women he was pursuing at the time, or on whom he was financially dependent. He even took one money from at least one lady, in return for good reviews of her work and help with her prosody. Whether this was more degrading than hack work for the magazines is difficult to judge, though Poe seems to have revolted periodically against the dependence.

Before their estrangement, he visited with Mrs Shew at her home on 10st Street, by Broadway. Poe was apparently distraught and suffering an acute sensitivity to sound, and the pealing of Grace Church nearby caused him deep distress. To calm him, Mrs Shew gave Poe a sheet of paper on which she wrote a title, "The Bells". They then seem to have collaborated on one of his most famous later poems – and another whose very rationale was to capture a single effect or impression – before Poe slept off whatever was ailing him and was taken back to Fordham. "The Bells", much revised, appeared in print a month after his death.

Somewhat earlier in the summer of 1848, Poe was in Lowell, Massachusetts, at the invitation of an admirer called Mrs Jane Ermina Starkweather Locke, with whom he had conducted a curious, manipulative correspondence, posing as the unapproachable widower but also leading her on with a great show of curiosity about her circumstances. He gave his lecture as planned and apparently without incident, but instead of paying suit to Mrs Locke he fell head over heels in love with her neighbour – and possibly kinswoman – Mrs

Nancy Locke Heywood Richmond; she became his "Annie", dedicatee of a passionate poem, and she provided him with a refuge when things were awry elsewhere.

Poe was in Providence in 1848 because of not one but two further women. Three years earlier, he had met a bright and pretty literary woman, just a couple of years younger than himself, called Mrs Frances Sargent Osgood. She had been given "The Raven" by its publisher and was equally captivated by its author, who continued to write to her when she went abroad to take a cure. The friends – and it seems they were platonic friends – paid a visit to Providence shortly after their meeting. It seems typical of Poe that when he was on the arm of one lady he should be smitten by another, though he had a mere glimpse of Mrs Sarah Helen Power Whitman standing on her veranda or in her garden. Poe was, of course, married to Virginia at the time and at least notionally faithful. Close upon his widowhood, though, he began a campaign to woo Mrs Whitman. She apparently rejected him, on grounds of her age – she was only six years older than Poe – and health, though these may have been gentle rationalisation of more profound problems. Mrs Whitman had been warned off Poe, and perhaps more important, her mother strongly opposed the relationship and Mrs Power controlled the family finances.

Poe was not to be denied, however. If Mrs Locke was his "Annie", then Mrs Whitman was his "Helen", similarly immortalised in verse, and he pursued her with a Faustian obsessiveness that seems more intellectual in origin – Mrs Whitman was a good poet – than erotic. In November 1848, after an inconclusive response to a repeated proposal of marriage, Poe appears to have half-heartedly attempted suicide, swallowing a non-lethal quantity of opium tincture, probably on top of a certain amount of alcohol, which he promptly vomited up again. He seemed to be staying with the Richmonds in Lowell at this point but later in the month he returned to Providence, apparently on the verge of collapse. He was treated, for "cerebral congestion", by a Dr William Pabodie, apparently a mutual friend, and it seems the threat of Poe's demise overcame Mrs Whitman's reservations for she agreed to become engaged, on condition that Poe abstained. It was a sympathetic gesture, rather than that of a woman in love.

Poe at the time was writing his lecture on "The Poetic Principle", which reiterates his belief that verse is nothing other than the "rhythmical creation of beauty". It is itself a beautiful piece of writing, more coolly argued and elegantly cadenced than earlier manifestos, though it rises to an ecstatic climax as Poe itemises the things that feed a poet's soul. Just as he had introduced an unexpected element of mysticism to *Eureka*, he here concedes that truth and moral effects may be part of poetry's substance, provided they are not made an occasion for didacticism. Thus, ideas of nobility may be a spur to writing verse, though subordinate to the beauty of the natural world, its sights sounds and smells, and entirely subordinate other than through the duties of chivalry to "the beauty of woman – in the grace of her step – in the lustre of her eye – in the melody of her voice – in her soft laughter – in her sigh – in the harmony of the rustling of her robes. He deeply feels it in her winning endearments – in her burning enthusiasms – in her gentle charities – in her meek and devotional endurances – but above all – ah, far above all – he kneels to it – he worships it in the faith, in the purity, in the strength, in the altogether divine majesty – of her *love*".

This is powerful and breathless stuff. If *Eureka* was a prose poem masquerading as a scientific treatise, the final pages of "The Poetic Principle" look less than a literary essay than a very public love letter: but to which woman? The text was only published after Poe's death, but it was given as a lecture – to a large audience this time – at Providence, where Poe must have become something of a celebrity, and certainly the object of scandalised curiosity. True to form, after delivering his text, he refreshed himself with some young male admirers and appeared at Mrs Whitman's the worse for drink, though on this occasion nothing dramatic happened and Poe's fiancée does not seem to have considered the conditions of their engagement broken.

The lecture was given on December 20th 1848, and two days later a document was drawn up in Providence to transfer certain finances to Mrs Whitman, in explicit preparation for her marriage to Edgar Allan Poe. In the event, the banns were not read and the engagement fizzled out in a series of strange, self-justifying letters – Poe's half of the correspondence survives – in which Poe seems to offer her every opportunity to call the marriage off. Given that at the same time he continued to woo "Annie" in passionate terms far more explicit than any addressed to his idealised "Helen", he was not wholeheartedly committed to anything other than securing financial security for himself. For "Annie", on the other hand, he had a physical passion, though her husband apparently never suspected Poe of any impropriety.

He may well have been apostrophising "Annie" in the peroration to "The Poetic Principle". He was certainly thinking of her when he used the name in "Landor's Cottage", his last published story, though it is typical of Poe's emotional double-dealing at the time that he should have suggested the same idyllic setting, based on the little house at Fordham, to Mrs Whitman as a place where *they* might experience a marriage of true minds.

Poe was still writing, and writing well. The other, better story of his final year is "Hop-Frog", a cruel revenge story in which a crippled court jester – is that how Poe now saw himself? – is plied with wine by his king but repays the insult by persuading his tormentor and other members of a sadistic court to dress as orang utans (that creature again!). The skins have been soaked in tar and Hop-Frog burns them all to death. So deeply embedded in the unconscious is some of Poe's imagery that one wonders if there is any connection between a further, minor act of cruelty, when the king dashes a glass of wine in the face of a kindly servant girl Trippetta, and an apparent incident in the unwinding of Poe's relationship with Mrs Whitman when she apparently put a handkerchief soaked in ether over her face. It in turn echoes his histrionic "overdose" of laudanum, one carefully calculated, one suspects, to be non-fatal.

∞∞∞

The shadow of Rufus Griswold falls heavily over everything that happens in this period. Poe himself thought sufficiently well of Griswold to appoint him his literary executor. Griswold's stewardship of the role was ambiguous in the extreme. He did, to be sure, guarantee that Poe's works were gathered together in a posthumous edition published in 1850, but by then he had already set in motion a myth of Edgar Allan Poe so powerful and pernicious that even after several generations of revisionist research and reassessment seems difficult to overturn.

On the day of Poe's funeral, an article, signed "Ludwig" appeared in the *New York Tribune* which began: "Edgar Allan Poe is dead. He died in Baltimore the day before yesterday.

The announcement will startle many, but few will be grieved by it". The author was soon revealed to be Griswold. He compounded the insult a year later with his "Memoir of the Author", which was included in the collected works and which presented Poe as a crazed drunk, addict and lunatic. Griswold's malice was only matched by his enterprise in creating the evidence for his damaging image of Poe. Many, and perhaps the majority of the letters he brought forward as evidence for his portrayal of Poe, have been proved to be clever forgeries, all of them so constructed as to present Griswold as a sympathetic and well-intentioned literary colleague, Poe as a maundering fool. He even distorts a relatively recent incident like Poe's tipsy behaviour after the lecture in Providence (surely one of the rare moments when a drink might have been justified) as a dramatic confrontation when no such thing is known to have taken place.

It is one of the strangest and also one of the most effective acts of literary assassination on record, and not even the presence of a smoking gun – or rather a file of reeking letters – has been able to reverse it.

ooooo

Poe's own decline seemed anything but irreversible at the beginning of 1849. He was still a practising journalist and still capable of writing effective verse. His last significant poem was "Annabel Lee", a delightful, ballad-like conception which seems to have been inspired by memories of Virginia. With exquisite irony, it appeared in the *New York Tribune* on the same day as the "Ludwig" obituary. Poe was still capable of effective polemical writing as well. In March, he published a review of James Russell Lowell's *Fable for*

Critics and expressed his dismay at an old friend's characteri-
sation of himself as two-fifths fudge. In a more disinterested
way, though, he was more concerned that Lowell seemed to
have ignored Southern writing. As his energies ebbed, he
seemed to turn ever more often to the South that had shaped
him. Political battle lines were also hardening in the pre-Civil
War period. Poe's suspicion of the abolitionists further alienated him in New York and New England. So it is significant
that the Lowell review should have appeared in the *Southern
Literary Messenger* where a new editor, John R. Thompson,
also accepted a new series of "Marginalia" from Poe, one of
the best of which looks movingly at the plight of a soul superior to its surroundings.

He received some sign of interest from an Illinois publisher,
who wanted to start up a literary magazine, but Poe could
not imagine becoming a literary figurehead in Oquawka. He
saw the future where he had spent a now curiously distanced
past, in Richmond. He started his journey at the end of June
1849, saying farewell for what turned out to be the last time
to Mrs Clemm, his gullible, meddling, foolishly fond mother-
in-law. He wrote to her again a week later from Philadelphia,
though he dates the letter as from New York. He claims to
have been imprisoned for drunkenness (never corroborated),
but protests that the cause was forgivable: "It was about Virginia". In the same letter, he repeats his wish to live no longer
after completing *Eureka*: "I must die". It sounds dramatic
or self-dramatising, but if Poe had suffered cholera as he
suggests – it is recorded in the city that summer – then he
wouldn't be the first to wish to die with those symptoms and
after-effects. While in Philadelphia Poe also met John Sartain,
who later published "The Bells". Sartain gives a muddled
and mostly self-serving account of a drunk, shabby figure

who talks obsessively about a *Pym*-like dream of a glowing female figure and a black bird. By this stage in the narrative, it scarcely requires much in the way of psychoanalytic training to explain such visions. Nor do we need to over-indulge outrage at the almost pathological embellishment of every story relating to Edgar Allan Poe at this time. In an age of emotional and descriptive surplus, feelings and facts were subject to sometimes grotesque elaboration, and proximity to a man of Poe's celebrity merely enhanced that tendency.

By mid-July Poe was established at a boarding house in Richmond, seemingly much improved and making something of a success of his visit. He gave "The Poetic Principle" as a lecture again and repeated his performance on September 24th. This time in Richmond he really did renew his romance with Sarah Elmira Royster. Their affair has the bittersweet quality of one resumed rather later in life, but it seems to have been genuine and Poe had sufficient charisma to convince Elmira that they might marry, though once again there is a hint that genuine affection was less strong than a desire to raise collateral for his *Stylus*.

Despite the apparent success, there is an underlying hint of hectic desperation. Poe was simultaneously romancing Mrs Anna Lewis, for whom he had performed literary favours for money. He had plans to do the same for a Mrs St Leon Loud in Philadelphia, and Mrs Clemm was badgering Griswold for help in return for good reviews. Just as the emotional tenor of correspondence from the time has to be adjusted for modern ears, so too, it is necessary to recalibrate standards of critical probity for the time. Such arrangements were hardly unique, but there is nonetheless an air of anxiety which certainly benefits from hindsight but which is palpable nonetheless.

∞∞∞

The manner of Edgar Allan Poe's death has attracted almost as much attention as his work; its medical cause has been obsessed over like Mozart's; it has even attracted that peculiarly American appetite for conspiracy theory. In the absence of a reliable autopsy, only tentative conclusions can be reached on the basis of a few eye-witness testimonies, but at various times tuberculosis, a heart seizure, meningitis, a recurrence of cerebral congestion or possibly cholera, chronic alcoholism, a suicidal drug overdose and even rabies have been adduced. Syphilis, a 19th century obsession similar to that of HIV/AIDS today, is rarely mentioned, curiously. It has even been suggested that Poe fell victim to a practice known as "cooping", in which potential voters were rounded up on an election day, plied with drink and then marched to one polling station after another to register multiple votes.

Whatever the case, death did not strike him out of a clear blue sky. At Poe's final reading of "The Poetic Principle" on September 24th, he looked pale and depressed. Elmira wrote to Mrs Clemm that two nights later Poe was feverish. She wanted him to postpone a journey back to New York, but he took the Baltimore boat the next morning. What happened to Poe over the next week is not reliably known. He seems to have gone on from Baltimore to Philadelphia, where there is evidence that he saw friends and contacts, and further evidence that his health was poor. The mystery is why, instead of moving on to New York, he went back to Baltimore.

That he did is the only certainty because on October 3rd 1849, a printer on the *Baltimore Sun* called Joseph W. Walker sent a message to a Dr Snodgrass to the effect that "There is a gentleman, rather the worse for wear, at Ryan's 4th ward polls, who goes under the cognomen of Edgar A. Poe, and who appears to be in great distress, & says he is acquainted with you ... " Snodgrass found him in a pub that had served as a polling place for that day's congressional ballot. At the very last, a family member, albeit a distant one, rallied to Poe's help. Henry Herring was the widower of Poe's aunt Elisabeth. He and Snodgrass took Poe to the Washington College Hospital. Neilson Poe sent clothes to replace the soiled ones, but did not visit. Poe was unconscious when admitted, but unable to explain his condition when he wakened in the early hours of the following day.

By Saturday, he had worsened and in the grip of his fever began to shout a name. Though speculation has fuelled many articles and internet discussions, the identity of "Reynolds" has never been satisfactorily established. Seventy-two hours after regaining consciousness in hospital, Poe's breathing changed. One tradition suggests that his last words were a whispered prayer, but such things are often consoling fictions. Perhaps he whispered "Eureka!" Around three o'clock in the morning on Sunday, October 7th 1849, Edgar Allan Poe became one with the universe again. It is not known who – or what – was there to greet him.

Chronology

YEAR	AGE	POE
1809	0	Born January 19th in Boston, Massachusetts, second son to David Poe and Elizabeth Arnold Poe; David Poe's last appearance on stage (October 18th), subsequent movements and date of death unknown
1810	1	Poe family resident in New York City and Richmond, Virginia; Rosalie Poe born (?December 20th)
1811	2	Poe family resident in Richmond, Charleston and Norfolk, VA; death of Elizabeth Poe in Richmond (December 12th)
1812	3	Poe fostered by John and Frances Allan; living in Richmond; Rosalie Poe seriously ill (December).
1813	4	First schooling in Richmond?
1816	7	At school in London, Mlle Dubourg's.
1817	8	Allans and Poe move to Southampton Row; business worsening.
1818	9	At the Reverend Dr John Bransby's school, Stoke Newington (to May 1820).
1819	10	Frances Allan suffers renewed ill health.
1820	11	Allans and Poe return to Richmond, via New York (arrived July 21st, August 2nd).
1821	12	Poe at school of Joseph H. Clarke, Richmond (to December, 1822).

OTHER

Births of Felix Mendelssohn (February 3rd) of Abraham Lincoln (February 12th); James Madison succeeds Thomas Jefferson as US President; death of Thomas Paine (June 8th), author of *Common Sense* (1776), a key text in the American split with the British Crown, and of *The Rights Of Man* (1791), a pamphlet on Enlightenment ideas; wearing of masks at balls in Boston forbidden by law (December 30th); Napoleonic Wars continue.

Birth of Margaret Fuller (May 23rd); King George III pronounced insane (porphyria).

Great Comet seen for much of year; Luddite riots in England (November).

Birth of Charles Dickens (February 7th); America imposes trade embargo with UK (April 4th); war declared between US and UK (June 18th); Napoleon invades Russia and is repelled (June – October).

Economic recession in UK; 'The Year Without A Summer', following the Mt Tambora eruption.

James Monroe becomes US President (March 4th); Elgin Marbles displayed in British Museum, less than half a mile from Southampton Row; Coleridge publishes *Biographia Literaria*.

Publication of *Frankenstein* (January 1st); US Congress adopts Stars and Stripes (April 4th).

Thomas Jefferson establishes University of Virginia; Walt Whitman born (May 31st); financial panic in US.

George IV succeeds to the British throne, ending the Regency (January 29th); James Monroe re-elected President (December 3rd).

Charles Baudelaire born (April 9th); Greek War of Independence (Poe claimed to have served).

YEAR	AGE	POE
1822	13	Virginia Clemm born (August 15th).
1823	14	Poe at school of William Burke, Richmond.
1824	15	Visit of Marquis de Lafayatte to Richmond (autumn); Poe a member of Junior Volunteers; ?meets Elmira Royster.
1825	16	Brief reunion with elder brother Henry; already writing verse.
1826	17	Enters University of Virginia, Charlottesville (February 14th); financial difficulties; leaves university and returns to Richmond (December).
1827	18	Travels to Boston (late March); enlists in US Army as 'Edgar A. Perry' (May 26th); publication of *Tamerlane and other poems* (early summer); posted to Fort Moultrie, Sullivan's Island, Charleston Harbour (October 31st, arrived November 18th, posting lasted until December 15th 1828.
1828	19	Promoted to artificer (May 1st).
1829	20	Promoted to sergeant-major (January 1st); death of Frances Allen (February 28th); Poe discharged and substituted from US Army (April 15th) *Al Aaraaf, Tamerlane and Minor Poems* published (December).
1830	21	Possibly in Richmond (to May); sat West Point entrance examination (late June, matriculated July 1st); John Allan remarries (October 5); continuing bad relations between Allan and Poe.
1831	22	Poe court-martialled for neglect of duty (January 28th, left February 19th); Poe moves to Clemm home in Baltimore; *Poems by Edgar A. Poe, Second Edition* published (April); death of Henry Poe (August 1st).
1832	23	First short stories published in *Philadelphia Saturday Courier* (January-December); John Allan's will provides for illegitimate children, but not for Poe (April 17th, codicils added December 31st, March 15th 1833).

Publication of Olbers' Paradox (see Poe's *Eureka*).

Death of Lord Byron at Missolonghi (April 9th).

John Quincy Adams become President (March 4th).

Death of Beethoven (March 26th).

Jules Verne born (February 8th).

Andrew Jackson succeeds John Quincy Adams as President (March 4th).

Gustav Doré born (January 6th).

YEAR	AGE	POE
1833	24	'MS Found in a Bottle' wins fiction prize in *Baltimore Saturday Visiter* (published October 19th); poems also published in *Visiter*.
1834	25	Growing affection between Poe and Virginia?; death of John Allan (March 27th).
1835	26	Working as assistant editor, *Southern Literary Messenger*; grandmother Mrs David Poe dies (July 7th); rumours – probably false – of secret marriage to Virginia in Baltimore (September 2nd); Poe warned about his drinking, reinstated at *Messenger* (September).
1836	27	Poe and Virginia Clemm marry in Richmond (May 16th); Poe attempts to make a claim on Mrs Clemm's behalf against Mrs David Poe's annuity (June); illness and further problems at the *Messenger* (November, December); writes many reviews and critical notices.
1837	28	Early instalments of *The Narrative of Arthur Gordon Pym* published (*SLM,* January, February); Poe leaves the magazine, travels to New York with Virginia and Mrs Clemm (February); *Pym* copyrighted by Harpers (June); William Burton founds *Gentleman's Magazine* (July).
1838	29	*Pym* published by Harpers (July) 'Ligeia' published in *American Museum* (September); does editing work on *The Conchologist's First Book* (winter).
1839	30	Becomes assistant editor, *Burton's Gentleman's Magazine* (June); publishes 'The Fall of the House of Usher' (September); republishes 'William Wilson' (October).
1840	31	Begins serialisation of 'The Journal of Julius Rodman' in *BGM* (January); Poe leaves magazine (June) with 'Rodman' incomplete; prospectus for *Penn Magazine* published in *Saturday Courier* (June 6th); *Tales of the Grotesque and Arabesque* published (November); George Rex Graham acquires *Burton's;* Poe publishes 'The Man of the Crowd' in *Graham's Magazine* (December).

Deaths of Marquis de la Fayette (May 20th) and Samuel Taylor Coleridge (July 25th); slavery abolished in British Empire (August 1st); suppression of Spanish Inquisition.

Halley's Comet visible (perihelion in November); President Andrew Jackson censured by Congress (March 27th); 'Mark Twain' born (November 30th); Great Fire of New York (December 16th-17th).

Charles Darwin returns to England on *Beagle* (October); foundation of the Transcendental Club, Boston; publication of Ralph Waldo Emerson's 'Nature'.

Martin Van Buren assumes US presidency (March 4th); Queen Victoria ascends British throne (June 20th); Louis Daguerre develops the daguerrotye (patented 1839).

'Trail of Tears': exile of the Cherokee nation (May 26th); death of American explorer William Clark (Lewis-Clark) (September 1st).

Birth of John D. Rockefeller (July 8th); Virginia Military Institute and American Statistical Association founded in Lexington and Boston respectively (both November).

United States claims Wilkes Land in Antarctica, following first circumnavigation by Capt. Charles Wilkes (January 19th); Province of Canada formed (July 23rd).

YEAR	AGE	POE
1841	32	Joins staff of *Graham's* (April); denies rumours of drinking (April 1st).
1842	33	Virginia suffers haemorrhage (January); Poe meets Charles Dickens in Philadelphia (March); leaves *Graham's* (probably May); James Russell Lowell announces *The Pioneer* (late summer); Poe seeks a post in the Tyler administration, but fails to appear for a meeting, perhaps drunk (mid-September).
1843	34	Lowell publishes 'The Tell-Tale Heart' (January); reaches an agreement with the proprietors of the *Saturday Museum* to underwrite his magazine in return for editorial work: unsuccessful (January); Lowell's *Pioneer* closes after three months; wins $100 from *Dollar Magazine* for 'The Gold Bug'.
1844	35	Moves to New York (April); 'The Balloon Hoax' published in *New York Sun* (April 13th).
1845	36	'The Raven' published in *Evening Mirror* (January 29th); establishment of *Broadway Journal*; 'The Imp of the Perverse' published in *Graham's* (July); *The Raven and other poems* published (November); Poe becomes half- and then outright owner of *BJ*, but forced to sell half-share again (December); 'The Facts of M. Valdemar's Case' published in *American Review* (December); first French translations appear.
1846	37	*BJ* ceases publication (January 3rd); 'The Philosophy of Composition' published in *Graham's* (April); 'The Literati of New York' begins publication in *Godey's Lady's Book* (May); 'The Cask of Amontillado' published in *Godey's* (autumn).
1847	38	Death of Virginia (January 30th); wins $225 damages in libel suit (February); reviews Hawthorne in *Godey's Lady's Book* (November).

OTHER

President William Henry Harrison dies (April 4th) after one month in office; succeeded by John Tyler; Charles Dickens concludes *Barnaby Rudge* in his periodical *Master Humphrey's Clock*.

Birth of Stéphane Mallarmé, later the author of 'Le tombeau d'Edgar Poe' (March 18th).

First meeting of Marx and Engels (August).

Potato famine begins in Ireland.

James K. Polk becomes 11th President of the US (March 4th); Henry David Thoreau begins his retreat at Walden Pond (July 4th); *Scientific American* begins publication (August 28th); Herman Melville's *Typee* published.

Pseudonymous publication of *Jane Eyre* and *Wuthering Heights* by Charlotte and Emily Brontë; death of Poe's contemporary Felix Mendelssohn (November 4th).

YEAR	AGE	POE
1848	39	Lectures 'On the Cosmography of the Universe' (i.e. *Eureka*) in New York (February 3rd); *Eureka* published by Putnam (June); 'The Rationale of Verse' published in *Southern Literary Messenger* (autumn).
1849	40	Returns to Richmond (July); discovered ill on streets of Baltimore and hospitalised (October 3rd); death of Edgar Allan Poe (October 7th).

California Gold Rush begins following discovery of gold at Coloma (from January); Karl Marx publishes *The Communist Manifesto* (February 21st).

Zachary Taylor becomes 12th President of the US, having refused to take his oath of office on the Sabbath (March 5th); potato famine ends in Ireland.

Index

A

"Al Aaraaf" (1829) 56–9,
 · 61, 65, 67, 77, 149
*Al Aaraaf, Tamerlane and
 Minor Poems* (1829)
 60
Allan, Frances ("Fanny")
 24–5, 28–9, 31–2, 36, 45,
 51–2
Allan, John 5, 21, 24–32,
 34–7, 39–45, 48, 50–3, 56,
 62, 73–5, 116
Allan, Louisa 52
"Annabel Lee" (1849) 160,
 162, 177
Arnold, Elizabeth *see* Poe,
 Eliza

B

Baltimore 6, 13–14, 17–18,
 21, 55, 61, 64, 67, 69, 71,
 73, 75, 86, 91, 95, 104,
 117, 159, 176, 180
Barrett, Elizabeth 145
Baudelaire, Charles 2, 102,
 169
"Berenice" (1835) 77–9, 82–3
Broadway Journal 6, 145–8,
 150–1, 153, 155
Bransby, Reverend John 33,
 35, 41
Brown, Charles Brockden 6,
 8, 129
Burton, William E 101, 103,
 105, 108–10, 112–13,
 115–17, 119–20, 122

C

Carey, Lee & Carey 77
Caroline, Queen 33–4
"The Cask of Amontillado"
 (1846) 156–8

Chivers, Thomas Holley
158–9, 162
"The City in the Sea" (1845)
66–7, 69, 114
Cleland, Thomas W 91–2
Clemm, George 21, 26
Clemm, Maria 55–6, 73,
91–2, 94, 107, 136, 147,
159–60, 169, 178–80
Clemm, Virginia 12, 55, 91,
107, 136, 159–60
Clemm, William 21, 55
Cooper, James Fenimore 6,
98, 109–10, 117, 135

D
Devereaux, Mary 73, 159
Dickens, Charles 106–7

E
"Eleanora" 124, 126
Ellis, Charles 33–4, 44
Emerson, Ralph Waldo 7,
121, 123
Eureka (1848) 9, 58, 139,
157, 163–9, 174, 181

F
"Fairyland" (1829) 59–60, 67
"Fall of the House of
Usher" (1839) 101, 104,
113–14

Freneau, Philip 7–8
Freud, Sigmund 3, 33, 65,
78, 152

G
Gentleman's Magazine
108–9, 111, 116, 119
"The Gold Bug" (1843) 49,
133–5, 142, 169
Gowans, William 94
Graham, George Rex
118–20, 127, 131, 133–4
Graham's 85, 101, 105, 118,
120–2, 125, 127, 130, 133,
142, 151, 155
Graves, Sergeant Samuel 51
Griswold, Rufus 9, 38, 49,
65, 109, 123, 126, 146–8,
151, 159, 160, 176–7, 179

H
Hawthorne, Nathaniel 6–7,
89, 120, 125, 129, 168
"Hop-Frog" (1848) 176
Hopkins, Charles 14–15, 19

I
Irving, Washington 6, 117

K
Kennedy, John Pendleton
71–2, 81–4, 88, 94, 119, 151

"King Pest" (1835) 75, 77, 80

"Lionizing" (1834) 77, 80, 83

L

Locke, Mrs Jane Ermina
   Starkweather 172–3

Longfellow, Henry
   Wadsworth 7, 89, 110, 115,
   117, 123, 144–5, 147–9

Lowell, James Russell 7, 10,
   115, 123, 130–2, 147, 149,
   177–8

M

Madison, James 4

Mallarme, Stephen 2, 102

Manor House School 32–3,
   35

"Manuscript Found In A
   Bottle" (1833) 29, 71–2,
   77, 97

"The Masque of the Red
   Death" (1842) 67, 75, 125

Melville, Hermann 6, 8,
   98–100, 102, 168

"Metzengerstein" (1832)
   71–3, 76

"Morella" (1835) 57, 77, 79,
   83, 104, 124

"The Murders in the Rue
   Morgue" (1841) 30, 32,
   122, 128, 131, 134

N

*The Narrative of Arthur
   Gordon Pym, of
   Nantucket* (1838) 2, 29,
   58, 96

Neal, John 61

O

Osgood, Mrs Frances
   Sargent 153, 173

P

Parrington, Vernon Louis
   1–3, 10

Penn Magazine 105, 118–19,
   131, 133, 142, 151

Phantasy-Pieces
   (unpublished) 79, 104,
   127–8, 134

"The Philosophy of
   Composition" (1846)
   141–3, 145, 162

"The Pit and the
   Pendulum" (1842) 128,
   130

Poe, David 16–23, 26, 55

Poe, Edgar Allan 1–10, 14,
   17, 34
   birth 4
   character and upbringing
      11–12, 22–5, 35–6
   death 181

England, time in 29–33
health 63, 129, 132, 180
literary background
    1–10, 39, 47, 141–3,
    145, 162
marriage 12, 55, 91, 107,
    136, 159–60
poetry 38, 45–53, 56–61,
    65–7, 69, 77, 114, 149
prose 2, 29, 58, 77–9,
    82–3, 96, 124, 126,
    128, 130,156–8
schooling 32–3, 35, 50,
    52, 54–5, 62–4, 69, 119
"Southern Gothic", and
    5–6, 30
Poe, Eliza 12–16, 18–24,
    28, 34
Poe, "General" 17–18, 23,
    36, 62, 73
Poe, Neilson 92, 94, 181
Poe, Rosalie 16, 22–3, 35, 39
Poe, William Henry 16, 20,
    23, 35, 39, 43, 73–5
Poems by Edgar Allan Poe:
    Second Edition (1831) 69
"The Poetic Principle"
    174–5, 179–80
Pound, Ezra 48, 58

Q
Quinn, Arthur Hobson 16,

19, 24, 34, 46, 48, 59–60,
    63, 82, 92, 99, 136, 146, 165

R
"The Raven" (1845) 9–10,
    121, 141–2, 145–6,
    148–50, 160, 162–3, 173
The Raven and Other
    Poems (1845) 151
Richmond 13, 15–16, 23–5,
    27–31, 34–40, 42, 44–6,
    48, 51–2, 56, 64, 73–4, 83,
    86, 91, 95–6, 171, 179
Richmond, Mrs Nancy
    Locke Heywood 172,
    174, 178
Royster, Elmira 37–8, 171,
    179

S
Scott, Sir Walter 6, 29–30,
    111, 122
"Shadow" 77, 79–80
Southern Literary
    Messenger 48, 82, 85,
    128, 144, 162, 178
Stanard, Mrs Jane Craig 37,
    68, 94

T
Tales of the Grotesque and
    Arabesque (1840) 111, 134

Tamerlane (1827) 45–8, 60, 161
"The Tell-Tale Heart" (1843) 131–2, 151
Thomas, Frederick W 118–20
Thoreau, Henry David 8
"To Helen" (1831) 37, 68–9
Twice-Told Tales (1837) 6, 89, 120

U

"Ulalume" (1847) 93, 160–4, 169
University of Virginia 37, 40–1, 43–5, 50

V

"The Valley of Unrest" (1831) 69

W

West Point 50, 52, 54–5, 62–4, 69, 119
White, Maria 130
White, Thomas Wylkes 82–7
Whitman, Mrs Sarah Helen Power 161, 173–6
Whitman, Walt 3, 6, 115
Williams, William Carlos 2–3, 5
"William Wilson" (1839) 29, 32–3, 41, 72, 101, 112–13, 131
Wirt, Professor William 60–1
Wyatt, Professor Thomas 107